INTEREST RATE
ANALYSIS
AND FORECASTING

INTEREST RATE ANALYSIS AND FORECASTING

DAVID KERN
PETER GUTMANN

WOODHEAD-FAULKNER

NEW YORK LONDON TORONTO SYDNEY TOKYO SINGAPORE

Published by Woodhead-Faulkner (Publishers) Limited,
Campus 400, Maylands Avenue
Hemel Hempstead
Hertfordshire HP2 7EZ
A division of
Simon & Schuster International Group

First published 1992

© Woodhead-Faulkner 1992

British Library Cataloguing in Publication Data
A catalogue for the book is available from the British Library

ISBN 0-85941-666-6

Typeset by Goodfellow & Egan Phototypesetting Ltd, Cambridge

Printed in Great Britain by BPCC Wheatons Ltd, Exeter

Contents

Preface

The rate of interest is a key economic variable which materially affects the circumstances of corporates and individuals. Knowledge of the role of interest rates and the reasons underlying their movements is crucial to an understanding of economic policy and financial developments.

This book is for students of the monetary system and financial markets, as well as for people involved at a more practical level with the economic and business scene. For people in business, whether small traders or corporate planners and financial controllers in major corporates, interest rates are a major factor determining risks and opportunities. A change, or expected change, in interest rates has important implications for the economy, and affects consumers' reactions as well as business investment decisions. The financial position of both individuals and companies is directly and immediately affected by movements in the level of interest rates. The main challenge for those involved in financial and business planning is to manage the risks associated with interest rate movements, and to balance them against other risks.

Identifying trends is a key part of this process, and an important element in the financial management of a company. The use of an analytical framework culminating in specific forecasts – both long- and short-term – and the availability of a systematic methodology for evaluating trends are essential for both the business planner and the financial decision-maker. This book aims to provide a coherent framework for this analysis.

The first two chapters deal with the theoretical framework for analysing absolute levels as well as movements in interest rates. Having set the foundations, we proceed in Chapters 3–5 to deal with some of the basic concepts relevant to the analysis of interest rates – inflation, maturity structure and risk. In Chapters 6–8 the impact of official policy and exchange rates is brought into the framework. Chapter 9 reviews interest rate history over the past three decades, focusing on the UK and the US, but also drawing on the experience of other countries, mainly Germany and Japan. The remainder of the book is concerned with forecasting interest rates – the establishment of a coherent forecasting framework (Chap. 10); the different techniques the forecaster can use (Chap. 11); and our view of the outlook for interest rates during the remainder of the decade (Chap. 12). Finally, there is a chapter outlining the values and dangers of forecasting.

David Kern
Peter Gutmann
London, February 1992

Acknowledgements

We are grateful to Dr Howard Archer of the Economics Section of National Westminster Bank's Market Intelligence Department for checking the text of this book and making many constructive comments; and to David Kern's secretary Mary Bailey, who has borne the burden of typing several revisions of the text, and whose speed, efficiency and accuracy in the face of other pressing demands are very much appreciated.

CHAPTER 1

The theoretical background

The theoretical background to interest rate determination provides a natural starting point to the more practical subjects of analysing market movements and of forecasting future trends in interest rates. The first part of this chapter looks at two different theoretical explanations of the determination of interest rates – one 'real' and the other 'monetary'. To be more precise, the main concern here is with the *general level of interest rates*. There are of course many different interest rates in a modern economy and much of this book will be devoted to explaining such variations according to the maturity, riskiness or currency denomination of the particular asset.

Both theories of the determination of the general level of interest rates start with the proposition that the rate of interest is a price; and, as with any other price, it is set by the interaction of demand and supply. Even at this early point of the analysis, there is a major divergence of thinking between the two theories, since the answer to the apparently simple question, 'demand and supply of what?' is by no means self-evident. The two theoretical frameworks start by providing different answers to this question. On the one hand, real theories of interest rates answer the question by focusing on investment (demand for funds) and savings (supply of funds). On the other hand, monetary theories make the rate of interest dependent on the demand for money (including speculative demand) and the money supply. These two theories of interest rate determination, which are outlined below, appear superficially to diverge sharply. However, these divergences can, in fact, be reconciled quite easily, and present no real difficulties for those involved in practical interest rate forecasting.

Real theories of interest

Explaining different theories entails the use of terminology which can often be a source of confusion. For example, real theories of interest rate determination discussed in this section are associated with monetarist thinking; in contrast, the monetary theory is generally preferred by Keynesians.

Real theories of interest were developed by classical economists in the 19th century and form an important element of current non-Keynesian or monetarist thinking. This approach – often called the loanable funds theory – argues that the real rate of interest (that is, the absolute, or nominal, level of interest rates adjusted for the rate of inflation) is determined by the interaction between, on the one hand, the supply of savings available for lending and, on the other hand, the demand for those funds to be borrowed and invested. The real rate of interest is crucial to interest rate analysis, and Chapter 3 has a more detailed explanation of this concept.

The supply of loanable funds is determined by the level of saving in the economy. This, in turn is determined by basic economic factors such as current and expected personal wealth and income, as well as a whole range of intangible factors including tastes, preferences and sociological attitudes. It is also influenced by the prevailing rate of interest. As with many other areas of economics, the relationships are complex, and the rate of interest is both determined by the supply of savings, as well as helping to determine it.

The demand for loanable funds is determined by the actual and prospective productivity of capital and the borrowing requirements necessary to close the gap between the level of desired capital investment and existing resources. As with the supply of loanable funds, the rate of interest is a key factor determining demand, since the amount borrowed will be determined by its cost, as capital equipment will be purchased only if the expected net return is greater than some acceptable minimum.

Thus, in the loanable funds analysis, the rate of interest is determined by the 'real' forces of savings and productivity. Because of its influence on each of these, the rate of interest also brings the supply of and demand for loanable funds into equilibrium. This important proposition is illustrated in Figure 1.1, where the demand and supply curves have widely accepted characteristics. The demand curve is downward sloping, indicating that the lower the rate of interest the greater the amount borrowed; while the supply curve is upward sloping, indicating that the higher the rate of interest the greater the amount saved. Only at interest

2

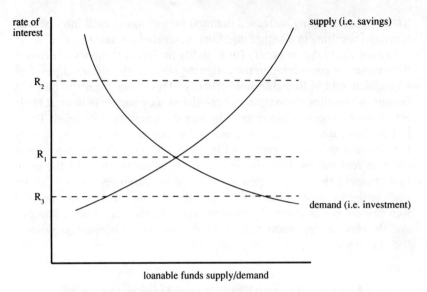

rate of interest

R_2

R_1

R_3

supply (i.e. savings)

demand (i.e. investment)

loanable funds supply/demand

Figure 1.1 Supply and demand for loanable funds.

rate R_1 are supply (i.e. savings) and demand (i.e. investment) in equilibrium. At any other interest rate, for example R_2 and R_3, there will be an imbalance. At R_2, the imbalance could reflect an excess supply of loanable funds, which market forces will eliminate due to falls in interest rates as individuals seek to deploy their surplus funds. At R_3, the imbalance might be due to excess demand for loanable funds. This excess demand would be gradually eliminated by the rise in interest rates, as prospective borrowers competed for the available (inadequate) supply of funds. As the interest rate rises, marginally profitable investment projects become unprofitable. At the same time, the rising interest rate would attract additional loanable funds, accelerating the pace at which saving equals investment.

The 'real' theory holds that interest rates change quickly and smoothly to produce equilibrium in the market, in response to changes in real economic factors. Such changes include, for example, shifts in saving habits which might result in reduced savings. In Figure 1.1, this would move the supply curve to the left (i.e. reducing the supply of savings at each interest rate level), resulting in higher interest rates. On the demand side, a change in interest rates might be the result of an increase in the productivity of new capital which would enhance the potential profitability of new investment. The resulting rise in the demand for loanable funds would shift the demand curve in Figure 1.1

3

to the right, implying increased demand for savings at each interest rate level and resulting in a higher equilibrium level of interest rates.

In contrast to the monetary (or liquidity preference) theory of interest determination considered in the following section, the money supply has no explicit role in loanable funds theory. This stems from the theory's origins in the classical system, where the money supply is neutral in its effect on the economy, determining only the absolute price level. Thus, in the classical system, an increase in the money supply will raise only the nominal values of saving and investment, and will exert no impact on their real values. It is also important to stress that one of the main limitations of the classical approach is that expectations – about factors such as the future productivity of capital or future levels of income and wealth – are not an integral part of the system, but such expectations can and do play an important role in the determination of interest rates in the real model.

The monetary or liquidity preference theory of interest rates

The monetary or liquidity preference explanation of interest rates is associated with Keynes. It emphasises the role of money, and rejects the classical approach's concentration on the rapid and smooth equilibrium between savings and investment which movements in interest rates are assumed to produce. In particular, Keynes focused on the potential for persistent disequilibrium, and on the risk of prolonged instability and speculation (ignored in the classical theory) which could result from the existence of very much larger stocks of monetary assets when compared with physical assets. Keynes highlighted the speculative role of expectations. He argued that even if interest rates are very low during a recession, people will still hold money rather than invest it, and so planned savings and investment levels need not be equal for a considerable period. His own approach, based on this tendency to hold money rather than to invest it during a depression – liquidity preference – was that interest rate levels are determined by the supply and demand for holding *money*, which entails a speculative element leading to long-term disequilibrium; rather than by the supply and demand for *investment funds*, which interest rates bring into equilibrium as in the classical loanable funds approach.

In Keynes's theoretical framework, money (i.e. liquid cash) is held not only for transaction and precautionary purposes, but also for speculative purposes. That is, money is held in preference to bonds to take advantage of the fact that if interest rates rise, bond prices will fall;

therefore there is a prospect of subsequently being able to purchase bonds at more favourable prices.

Conversely, if there are general expectations of a fall in interest rates and a corresponding rise in bond prices, people will prefer bonds to money. Thus, the demand for holding cash for speculative purposes is closely related to expectations regarding future rates of interest. The liquidity preference explanation for interest rate determination concentrates on the demand for money, laying particular emphasis on the speculative motive for switching between bonds and cash.

The theory also assumes that the money supply is determined independently by the authorities. The effect on interest rates of a change in the money stock in the liquidity preference theory is illustrated in Figure 1.2. Here, an increase in the supply of money from M_1 to M_2 will move the rate of interest from R_1 to a lower level, R_2. As the money supply increases in this example, investors will use the extra funds to buy securities, pushing up prices and reducing yields, thus exerting downward pressure on the general level of interest rates.

An important aspect of the liquidity preference analysis is that the speculative motive for holding money depends on both the current level of interest rates and expectations of future movements in interest rates. This traditional Keynesian proposition has been modified in more recent versions of the theory, because future nominal rates of interest will depend on changes in the expected rate of inflation over time. The

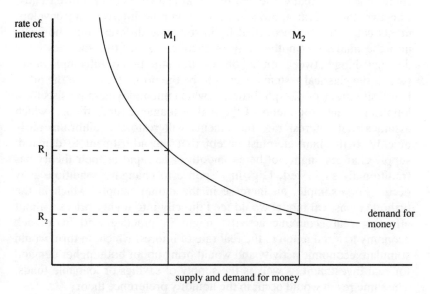

supply and demand for money

Figure 1.2 Effect of an increase in the money supply

amended version recognises that expectations of future movements in interest rates are guesses which may turn out to be wrong, and investors know this. Their uncertainty about the future leads them to hedge their financial portfolio positions, by holding some liquid assets, investing some funds short term, and investing some long term. This more sophisticated version of the liquidity preference theory may produce different demand curves for liquid funds; but does not alter the key role of expectations in determining the absolute level of interest rates. In addition, it is appropriate to mention here that expectations will also affect the term structure of interest rates as discussed in Chapter 4, *The interest rate yield curve*.

Reconciliation of the real and liquidity preference theories

Each of the two theoretical accounts of interest rate determination attempts to provide an analytical framework for explaining practical conditions in the financial markets. The fundamental issues on which the two theories differ are: (1) the role of the money supply; and (2) whether only real factors are relevant in determining the level of interest rates. However, these differences need not cause concern to the practical financial forecaster, who is interested in interpreting observed conditions in the real world and then taking a view about future trends. The two theoretical approaches for explaining interest rate developments can often be reconciled by introducing different time horizons into the analysis. Another way of reconciling the two theories is by distinguishing between, on the one hand, a situation of full employment (which the classical system assumes to be the normal) and, on the other hand, situations of disequilibrium in which unemployment persists for a long time. The proponents of the real or loanable funds theory, which assumes that interest rate movements will restore equilibrium fairly quickly to the market, must accept that the adjustment to demand/supply changes might not be as smooth or as rapid as their theory has traditionally suggested. Lags in response to changing conditions may occur. For example, an increase in the money supply, which in the orthodox classical model would feed directly into higher prices without affecting real economic activity, might in practice lead in a slack economy to a reduction in the real rate of interest which, in turn, would stimulate economic activity and would bring about both higher demand for real investment as well as the supply of savings or loanable funds. The same result would occur in the liquidity preference theory.

For their part, most Keynesians would accept that an increase in the money supply will, in the long term, raise the price level above what it otherwise would have been. While the short-term effect of an increase in the money supply is a reduction in interest rates and higher economic activity, the long-term effects are largely in terms of higher prices, while the initial stimulatory impact on activity gradually wears off as the system moves back to full employment. This is because, as prices rise, the demand for transaction and precautionary money balances will increase, thus tending to push interest rates up again.

Short- and long-term interest rates

While the two theories considered above provide explanations of the general level of interest rates, they are not sufficient to explain the movement of rates along the spectrum from very short to very long-term rates. The impact of government actions is always more powerful on short-term rates, although the close linkages between various financial markets mean that changes in short-term rates generated by the authorities' money market intervention are felt along the whole interest rate spectrum. Nevertheless, it is quite possible for this transmission effect to be weak or even perverse, so that the term structure of interest rates becomes distorted. For example, the Bank of England's intervention in the money markets can ensure an appreciable increase in short-term rates. However, if forces at the longer end are in equilibrium, and nothing changes to disturb the balance between demand and supply, then long-term rates could remain below short-term rates. Indeed, if a rise in short-term rates signals a more forceful anti-inflation policy, long rates could fall. This will distort the normal shape of the interest rate structure, which shows long-term rates at higher levels to compensate for greater risk and uncertainty, and for loss of liquidity.

In other words, while the government can exercise a strong influence over short-term interest rates in liberalized market places such as the UK, longer-term rates are largely determined by the basic demand/supply forces discussed earlier in this chapter, as well as by the impact of expectations about inflation analysed in Chapter 3. Even at the short end of the interest rate spectrum, however, government influence does not amount to full control. The money markets cannot be divorced from the fundamental demand/supply and expectational factors determining interest rates. If the markets consider that the interest rates the authorities are aiming at are unrealistic, there will be resistance. Alternatively, the markets may react to developments before the authorities do, either anticipating government action or forcing the authorities to intervene in order to regain control over interest rates.

Conclusion

The basic factors which market players observe and analyse when forecasting interest rate movements fit naturally into the two theoretical frameworks outlined above. A combination of 'real' and 'monetary' market forces – the supply of savings, the demand for investment, the supply of money and the various forms of demand for money – can explain in general terms how interest rates are determined. However, both the average level of interest rates as well as movements of specific interest rates at any particular moment are also determined by a multitude of factors ranging from wars, political crises and, above all, government monetary and exchange rate policy. Later chapters focusing on relevant areas of the financial environment will discuss these practical aspects in detail.

CHAPTER 2

Flow of funds analysis

The flow of funds system of accounts provides a comprehensive framework for identifying financial flows between the main economic sectors. The results are useful in analysing the relationship between different parts of the economy, as well as in examining the effects on the financial markets and on asset prices of the surpluses or deficits generated by each of the sectors. There are clearly important implications for interest rate analysis and forecasting in these financial and monetary links. This chapter outlines the flow of funds accounts and explains their relevance to interest rate analysis and forecasting.

Sector financial balances

The flow of funds analysis divides the economy into broad divisions, for each of which outflows of payments and inflows of receipts are identified. A typical statement of financial balances shows the *net aggregate position* of each sector vis-à-vis other sectors, and disregards flows within each sector. The five sectors considered, which taken together encompass the entire structure of a typical developed economy such as the UK, are shown in Table 2.1. The figures are the net financial balances of the UK sectors in recent years. The composition of each of these sectors is described on pages 11 and 12. Portraying a structure of financial balances between the main economic sectors, as shown in Table 2.1, imposes a discipline in the analysis of financial developments. The sum of the financial balances for the five economic sectors which make up the entire economy must by definition equal zero; and the forecaster is compelled to take explicit account of each sector's performance on other sectors in the economy. The flow of funds accounts thus provide a useful frame-

9

Table 2.1　Financial balances in the UK, 1987–90

£bn	Public sector	Personal sector	Companies	Financial institutions	Overseas sector*	Residual error
1987	−4	−5	−1	+4	+5	+1
1988	+7	−13	−9	+1	+15	−1
1989	+6	−4	−25	+4	+19	0
1990	+2	+7	−27	+4	+14	0

*The current account of the balance of payments with the sign reversed.

work which can be used to trace the broad effects of various policy measures throughout the economic system. For example, one can use flow of funds analysis to assess how various sectors respond to a credit squeeze by adjusting their financial positions.

As the UK economy moved into recession during 1989 and 1990, following the sharp increase in interest rates, the corporate sector experienced a massive deterioration in its financial position; this reflected reduced margins, weakening domestic demand and lower overseas earnings. The implication of the worsening company sector's financial position was that other sectors were collectively improving their financial balances, either reducing their deficits or increasing surpluses. The main transformation was in the personal sector, which moved from a record deficit in 1988 to a surplus in 1990, largely due to a significant reduction in borrowing and an increase in savings.

Flow of funds accounts identify and measure all the main net sources and uses of funds for each broad sector, including various financial instruments taking into account income receipts and expenditure on both physical as well as financial assets. The analysis can be used to trace important policy changes. For example, Table 2.2, the detailed flow of funds table, indicates in line 7 that the corporate sector increased its bank borrowing very substantially in 1989 in line with its changing financial position. This resulted in a sharp upsurge in money supply growth and subsequently brought about a significant tightening in monetary policy in that year.

There are a number of important definitional and data collection problems associated with flow of funds analysis. These stem largely from the fact that the quality of statistical reporting by the personal, corporate and overseas sectors is often flawed, and the precise borderlines between the various sectors are often very untidy. These problems inevitably mean that the application of the flow of funds approach can involve difficult problems. Nevertheless, the accounts provide a valuable framework for investigating past performance of the main economic sectors, for checking the results obtained using other analytical approaches, and for ensuring consistency in forecasting.

Definitions of the economic sectors

Public sector

In the UK, the public sector is made up of central government, local authorities and public corporations. Each of these sub-sectors could be treated separately, but they are usually taken together – partly for historical reasons, but mainly because the central government's policies dominate the behaviour of the rest of the sector. Central control is exercised through public expenditure programmes, responsibility for taxation (including local authority finance), centralized wage bargaining, pricing policies, subsidies and so on. Moreover, fiscal policy reflects the needs of the entire public sector; and the sector's net financial position or its borrowing requirement constitutes both the main expression of fiscal policy as well as an important ingredient of monetary policy. In some countries, nationalized industries are included in the corporate sector. In contrast, in the UK the financial arrangements of public corporations have historically been intimately connected with the central government and they have been treated as part of the public sector. However, the rapid privatization programme undertaken over the past decade has resulted in a rapid decrease in the size of this element in the public sector.

Personal sector

Conceptually, the personal sector is made up of 'households' or 'consumers'. Unfortunately, the statistical limitations of most UK official data makes it necessary to include charities and unincorporated businesses, such as farmers and various professionals (e.g. lawyers and accountants) in the official definition of the 'personal sector'. Although the household sector is predominant within the UK personal sector, the business and charities portion is not insubstantial, and exhibits different financial behaviour in both investment decisions and in its capital market activities, than do individuals. While this detracts somewhat from the analytical usefulness of any assessment of personal sector behaviour, the existing statistical definition still provides a very powerful analytical tool.

11

Industrial and commercial companies

Non-financial companies are treated as one single group, and it is not the purpose of flow of funds analysis to examine the behaviour of individual industries. Companies involved in finance-related activities (such as leasing or property) but which are not financial institutions are also defined as industrial and commercial companies.

Financial institutions

This sector comprises two major sub-sectors which for some purposes can be treated entirely separately, but which for broad macro-economic analysis can be satisfactorily unified. The first sub-sector, banks and building societies, is fairly homogenous; the second, other financial institutions, is more diverse and includes insurance companies, pension funds, investment and unit trusts, factoring companies and miscellaneous specialist financial institutions.

Overseas sector

Non-residents taken as a group are included in this sector and the financial accounts describe the transactions between them and the domestic sectors. The combined net financial deficit of the domestic sectors is the current account deficit of the UK as a whole, and this is also by definition the financial surplus of the overseas sector. Conversely, the financial deficit of the overseas sector is the current account surplus of the UK and reflects the combined net financial surpluses of the individual sectors.

Sectoral flow of funds analysis

For each of the economic sectors outlined above, the flow of funds accounts show financial transactions within a consistently defined system. The accounts of each sector identify and measure the main sources and uses of its funds, not only for physical goods and services but also for financial instruments; the accounts therefore encompass net borrowing and lending as well as the acquisition of financial assets and liabilities. In order to illustrate the analytical uses of the flow of funds approach, a somewhat simplified version of the 1989 sectoral accounts for the UK is shown in Table 2.2.

The presentation of sectoral flow analysis necessarily involves a vast array of figures, even in the simplified version shown in Table 2.2. A

Table 2.2 Flow of Funds in the UK (1989)

£ million	Public sector	Personal sector	Corporate sector	Financial institutions	Overseas sector	Sums of lines
1 Financial surplus/deficit*	6000	−4000	−25000	4000	19000	0
2 Cash	−1200	800	70	300	30	0
3 Bank/building society deposits	−200	40000	15000	−96800	42000	0
4 Treasury bills	−3000	–	800	1300	900	0
5 Gilt-edged stock	18300	−3100	−200	−13100	−1900	0
6 Other public sector	−4700	−1800	2100	−400	4800	0
7 Bank lending†	–	−13700	−35700	80600	−31200	0
8 Other lending	1800	−34700	−7900	33000	7800	0
9 UK company securities	4500 ⎰	−17400	2800	−400	19500 ⎱	0
10 Overseas securities	⎱	1000	13800	27300	−42100 ⎰	0
11 Unit trusts and pension funds	–	29000	–	−29000	–	0
12 Net foreign investment	–	–	−4000	900	3100	0
13 Accruals adjustment	–	3600	−100	−3500	–	0
14 Total identified financial transactions‡	6500	3700	−13330	200	2930	0
15 Balancing item	−500	−7700	−11670	3800	16070	0

*Broadly speaking, this is the sector's revenue less expenditure adjusted for investment and stockbuilding

†Excludes public sector (included in line 6)

‡The sum of lines 2 to 13

Source: Financial Statistics – Central Statistical Office

few explanatory remarks will be helpful before we highlight the broad relationships which emerge. Line 1 of the table shows each sector's net financial surplus or deficit. This is defined in the national accounts as the difference between each sector's savings and its investment expenditure on physical assets and stocks. The counterpart of this difference is shown in lines 2 to 13. These detail the individual financial transactions with their appropriate sign, and the sum total of all the financial transactions is shown in line 14. The convention is to give each transaction the same sign as its impact on the net financial balance of the entire sector. Thus, a net financial deficit as recorded, for example, by the corporate sector in the table is shown with a negative sign, and so are transactions representing net sales of assets and net increases in liabilities. This practice reflects the fact that lower assets and/or increased liabilities contribute to the sector's financial deficit. For example, the negative sign preceding the £35 700 million in line 7 indicates an increase in borrowing from banks.

Another important aspect of flow of funds accounts is that they have to obey by definition two very powerful balance sheet constraints. Firstly, the horizontal sum of each row in the table must add up to zero. Put differently, the sum total of the financial positions for the various sectors in each market (e.g. unit trusts in line 11 or government securities in lines 4 and 5) adds up to nil. Secondly, the vertical sum of the individual identifiable flows (line 14) for each sector theoretically equals that sector's net financial surplus or deficit (line 1). In practice, the problems inherent in collecting data mean that many of the figures are estimated only roughly, and this produces a discrepancy between totals which in theory should be equal. It is therefore inevitable that some residual error (or balancing item), which on occasion can be very large, is necessary to reconcile the columns.

Sectoral financial behaviour

Figure 2.1 provides useful background details for an examination of sectoral financial trends over the long term. The financial balances, as shown in line 1 of Table 2.2, are tracked for the past twenty years. The main net saver in the economy with funds to on-lend to other sectors, has traditionally been the personal sector. This sector had a substantial surplus until the late 1980s; this largely financed the public sector's persistent deficit as well as the occasional deficit of the corporate sector. The figure highlights the very sharp change in sectoral financial behaviour in the late 1980s. The personal sector moved into very large deficit, reflecting substantial borrowing, much of it due to the extraction

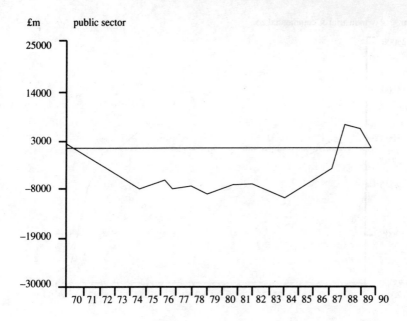

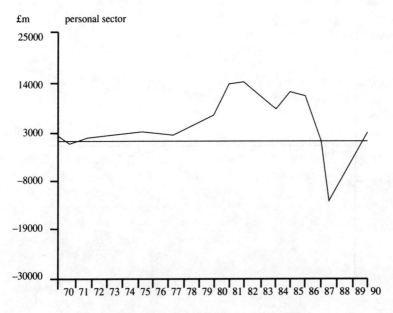

Figure 2.1 UK sectoral financial balances: 1970–90

15

FLOW OF FUNDS ANALYSIS

£m   industrial & commercial co.

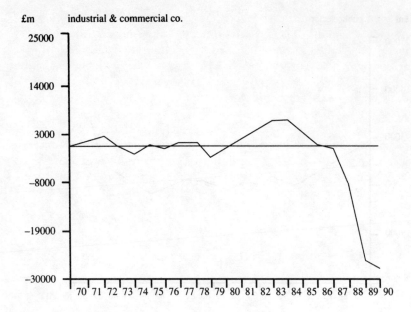

£m   overseas sector

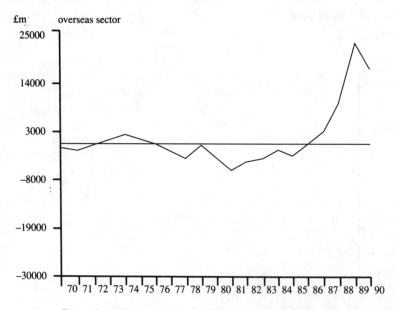

Figure 2.1 UK sectoral financial balances: 1970–90 (continued)

16

of significantly higher housing equity and its usage for increased consumer spending. The corporate sector also moved into record deficit. Initially, this was stimulated by expectations of continuing strong growth in domestic demand, which led companies to expand investment sharply in 1987, 1988 and 1989. However, starting in the autumn of 1989 and through 1990, the huge corporate sector deficit reflected high interest rates and the sharp cutback in personal sector spending. The counterpart of these shifts into sizeable deficit of both the personal and corporate sectors was the emergence of a public sector surplus for the first time in two decades. In addition, a massive surplus was registered by the overseas sector, which was equal to the combined deficit of the various domestic sectors. As explained earlier, this was equal to the UK's huge current account deficit.

Implications for interest rates

The major shifts in sectoral balances shown in the previous section had important consequences for UK interest rates. One result of the public sector moving from deficit to surplus was to relieve pressure on long-term rates, by removing the public sector as a competitor in the market for long-term funds. The large fiscal deficits of the early and mid-1980s were financed largely by issues of new gilts. The public sector surpluses of the late 1980s resulted in a marked reduction in demand for long-term funds and an accompanying reduction in pressure on long-term interest rates.

At the same time, the private sector's deficits were largely financed by the banks and the building societies and this put upward pressure on short-term interest rates. This shift in the private sector's financial position from traditional surplus to (at least temporary) substantial deficit exacerbated inflationary pressures and worsened the UK's external deficit. It ultimately triggered drastic actions by the authorities to curb the unsustainable consumption boom, with short-term rates being raised very sharply to levels well above those produced by natural demand/supply pressures. This official action had the additional effect of helping to attract the substantial amounts of foreign capital, mainly portfolio, to finance the large current account deficit incurred in recent years.

These developments, a combination of reduced pressure in the long-term markets and increased pressure boosted by official action to raise short-term rates sharply, produced after the autumn of 1988 a sharply downward-sloping interest rate yield curve. This concept is discussed in detail in Chapter 4.

Conclusion

The identification of sectoral deficits and surpluses through the flow of funds approach gives the analyst an insight into some of the factors which affect interest rate movements. The flow of funds provides a useful framework for analysing past events and for helping to establish broad relationships which can be used as a tool for forecasting. However, sectoral financial balances cannot be used in a mechanistic way. It is important to distinguish clearly between the accounting identities which ensure that on the one hand the deficits of some sectors are always reflected in equal surpluses incurred by other sectors and, on the other hand, the dynamic market relationships which reconcile initial imbalances between the sectors through changes in economic policy and in the level of interest rates.

CHAPTER 3

Interest rates and inflation

The rate of inflation is a factor of crucial importance to the analysis and forecasting of interest rates. Inflation impacts on interest rates in a number of significant ways. The starting point is that, in general, the rate of interest can be defined as consisting of two elements – inflation and the real rate of interest. In other words, the rate of inflation is a major component of the actual, or nominal, level of interest prevailing at any particular time.

Some may regard this distinction between nominal and real rates as somewhat artificial. However, the gap between the actual interest rate level and inflation (i.e. the real rate) is a highly meaningful measure of the true burden of interest rate costs facing individuals and companies. As well as being significant at a practical business level, the real rate of interest is a key measure of the toughness of monetary policy. During the 1980s, interest rates emerged as the dominant monetary policy instrument used by governments to control inflation. More specifically, in pursuing counter-inflationary policies, the authorities vary the level of short-term interest rates, either in order to influence intermediate targets such as money supply growth and credit expansion, or as a more direct weapon in order to dampen domestic spending.

More recently, partly because domestic money supply targets proved ineffective and partly in reaction to wider policy aims such as the establishment of European economic and monetary union (EMU), exchange rate stability has become a key counter-inflation weapon. In such circumstances, the monetary authorities will vary the level of interest rates in order to produce a desired exchange rate level. For example, a country with strong inflationary pressures or a weak external balance will counter the adverse impact on its exchange rate by raising interest rates. This chapter will focus on the various relationships between inflation and interest rates.

Nominal and real rates of interest

The nominal rate of interest is defined as the actual rate quoted by the lender and paid by the borrower expressed as a percentage per annum of the principal. In analysing the effect of interest rate changes, either on investment decisions or on consumer spending, the nominal rate needs to be adjusted to take account of inflation. That is, it is necessary to consider the 'real' rate of interest to understand fully the true impact of interest rate developments.

The real rate of interest can be calculated simply by deducting the inflation rate – as measured, say, by the Consumer Price Index (CPI) in the US or the Retail Price Index (RPI) in the UK – from the nominal or quoted rate. Thus, if in a given year a bank deposit offered 10% per annum, and the RPI was 5% during the year, the depositor received a real return of 5%. To be strictly accurate calculation must be through division rather than subtraction. The precise formula is:

$$\frac{100 + \text{ the nominal rate of interest (say 10)}}{100 + \text{ the rate of inflation (say 5)}} \times 100 - 100$$

In the above example, $\dfrac{110}{105} \times 100 - 100$

gives a real rate of 4.8%. When the inflation rate is below 10% it is perfectly safe to use the approximation of subtracting the inflation rate from the nominal rate. However, for larger figures the more accurate formula using division should be applied.

The real rate of interest is of major significance in evaluating the true burden of interest rates on individuals and companies and, therefore, in assessing the likely effect of the authorities' attempts to influence behaviour through interest rate policy. For example, if the inflation rate in a country is equal to the rate of interest at which much personal borrowing takes place, even a very high nominal rate, let us say 25%, is hardly likely to dampen demand for credit. Similarly, investors will not be satisfied with the return they receive in real terms. A nominal rate of 25% will be unattractive, if the inflation rate is higher still, as the interest payment received would be insufficient to maintain the capital value in real terms of the financial asset, and purchasing power at the end of the investment period would be less than at the outset.

If the nominal rate of interest is higher than inflation, then the real rate of interest is said to be positive. This situation is the more normal one, since the rate of return expected by investors would, in general, be

20

higher than inflation. However, real rates can be negative, either on individual transactions, or across the spectrum of borrowing and lending in the economy. This occurs in situations where inflation is higher than the general level of interest rates. In the case of the UK, this occurred on a number of occasions in the 1970s.

The method shown above for calculating real interest rates uses current inflation figures. However, one fundamental difficulty is that the real rate of interest on an investment or a loan is determined by the rate of inflation prevailing over the duration of the transaction and *not* by the current or past rate. Thus, where the nominal rate of interest is guaranteed, for example on a fixed interest security, the real rate for that security would be the nominal (guaranteed) rate minus the *expected* rate of inflation. It should be borne in mind that, when applied to forward-looking investment decisions, the calculation of real interest rates always involves an element of forecasting *future* inflation rates. Past or current rates of inflation can only be used as a guide or an approximation. There are two additional specific difficulties in the analysis and calculation of forward-looking real interest rates: (1) different investment projects relate to different periods and entail, therefore, different expected inflation rates; and (2) different individuals will hold, at any moment in time, very different views about future inflation.

Real interest rates and economic policy

Given that the real rate of interest determines the true burden imposed on individuals or companies, it is clear that for monetary policy to be effective in dampening inflationary pressure, it will be necessary not only to raise nominal interest rates, but to ensure that real interest rates also rise. The techniques used by the authorities to achieve the required level of short-term interest rates are described in Chapter 7. In this chapter, we undertake a historical review of real interest rate levels seen in a number of countries in the past three decades. The swings in real rates over the period, from positive to negative and back to positive, closely reflect significant developments in the financial background, notably changes in policy stances over the period.

Figures 3.1–3.3 show the pattern of real rates in the UK, the US and West Germany expressed in five-year averages since 1960. In the US and the UK, there was a particularly stable relationship between interest rates and inflation during the 1960s, with a real interest rate of around 1% and 1.5% respectively throughout the decade. This stability reflected the fact that the world was still operating relatively successfully

21

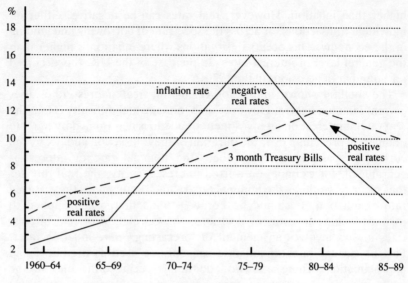

Figure 3.1 UK real interest rates, 1960–89.

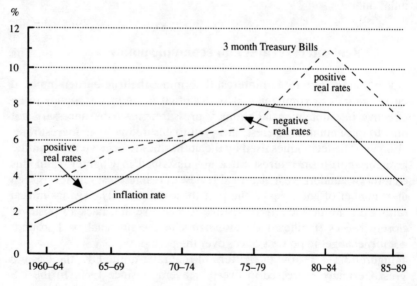

Figure 3.2 US real interest rates, 1960–89

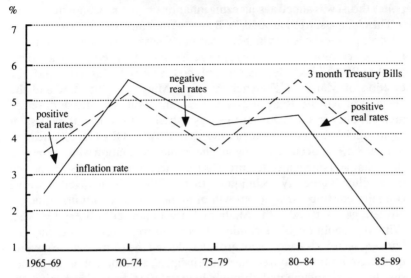

Figure 3.3 West German real interest rates, 1965–89.

under the Bretton Woods system of fixed exchange rates, which combined sustained moderate growth and relatively low inflation.

The situation changed radically during the 1970s, following the breakdown early in the decade of the Bretton Woods system of semi-fixed exchange rates and the effects of the 1973/74 oil crisis. This first sharp oil price rise of the 1970s will be referred to as OPEC 1 (OPEC is the Organisation of Petroleum Exporting Countries, the oil cartel which dominated the oil market at that time). The combined impact of floating exchange rates and sharply increased energy prices was to push inflation rates to historically high levels. At the same time, economic policy in the aftermath of OPEC 1 was mainly designed to counteract the risk of recession, which most governments regarded then as a more serious threat than inflation. The inevitable consequence was that the inflationary impact of the oil price rise was accommodated without resistance by policy makers, and higher inflation became entrenched in the economic system for several years. Indeed, it was not until the late 1970s, when strong political pressures against the inflationary upsurge started to build up, that the policy stance changed and greater reliance was placed on tight monetary policy to control inflation by curbing demand. Interest rates rose much more slowly than inflation during most of the 1970s, a period characterized by negative real rates reflecting a policy stance which largely accommodated inflation. However, the position was reversed dramatically in the 1980s when the main

23

policy thrust was aimed at squeezing inflation out of the economic system.

The change started around 1978 as governments became aware of the adverse political costs of higher inflation. The switch to a more counter-inflationary 'monetarist' policy approach was symbolized by the appointment of Paul Volcker as Chairman of the US Federal Reserve (Fed), the election of Margaret Thatcher as Prime Minister in the UK and the election of Ronald Reagan as US President. Following these developments, policy in OECD countries was tightened to cope with persistent rapid inflation, which had been exacerbated by the OPEC II oil price rise in 1979/80. This occurred following the Iranian revolution which removed the Shah, and one major feature was that increased emphasis was placed on resolute monetary techniques. In the UK, this involved a strong commitment to control the growth of money supply, with firm quantitative targets set under the Medium-Term Financial Strategy (MTFS). With the abolition of remaining direct controls over credit, the UK banking sector's balance sheet growth reflected the Conservative government's commitment to free market principles, and control of the money supply was implemented through high interest rates dampening the demand for lending and money. Three-month rates in the UK rose very sharply from an average 8% in 1978 to 15% in 1980. The high priority given to reducing inflation was also reflected in much higher interest rates in the US, with 3-month rates rising from an average 6% in 1978 to over 14% in 1980.

The 1980s were characterized by large capital movements and considerable volatility in interest and exchange rates. Financial imbalances, particularly the US's budgetary and external deficits, rose to levels considered destabilizing. Against this background, although inflation fell steadily in the early 1980s both in the US and the UK, interest rates remained high in both nominal and real terms. As well as helping to finance the various global imbalances and supporting exchange rate stability, high interest rates were in themselves a key ingredient of the anti-inflation stance. Volatility in interest rates was much less dramatic in low inflation countries such as Germany and Switzerland, but rates remained high in real terms in these countries as well. In the UK, although the budgetary position moved into surplus after 1988, interest rates were again raised sharply to curb excessive private sector spending and borrowing, and thus relieve pressure on inflation and the current account. While inflation rose strongly between 1988 and 1990, from 5% to over 9%, real interest rates remained very high by historical standards given the high level of nominal rates (over 15% for 3-month money).

Inflation, exchange rates and interest rates

The fact that inflation rates in various countries can differ systematically over time is a major factor in determining interest rate and exchange rate movements. Over very long periods, there is a very close correlation between inflation differentials, interest rate differentials and currency movements (see Chap. 8). While there are numerous examples of the currency of a country with above-average inflation appreciating in the short term, an analysis over long periods perhaps seven years or more will almost invariably show a strong link between relative rates of inflation and relative currency movements. One reason why the relationship does not hold in the short term is that a country may attempt to prevent a devaluation of its currency – and thereby avoid exacerbating inflationary pressures – by keeping interest rates high to attract short-term investment. While this policy may delay a currency depreciation and may even mitigate it by acting as a powerful anti-inflation antidote, it is unlikely to be totally effective in the face of a persistently and significantly unfavourable inflation differential. Nevertheless, the relative success of countries with high inflation, such as Ireland and Italy, in reducing their inflation rates within the framework of the Exchange Rate Mechanism (ERM) of the European Monetary System (EMS) shows the positive potential of such a policy.

As far as the relationship between interest rates and exchange rates is concerned, it is important to separate the technical link, which is expressed in the forward exchange rate, and the more fundamental connection. In general, countries with high inflation will have weak currencies, and will require relatively high interest rates to compensate for the potential future devaluation of their currencies. However, a rise in interest rates in a particular country can sometimes be the first stage in the corrective mechanism towards reducing inflation and strengthening the currency. Therefore, one must always use judgement in interpreting the reasons for a rise in interest rates. In countries with chronic high inflation and weak currencies (e.g. Latin America) high interest rates are usually a belated and inadequate compensation for these weaknesses. However, in the US, most of Western Europe and Japan, high interest rates have often been an important ingredient in the policy response which, if pursued resolutely, can help to reduce inflation and strengthen the currency.

Inflation and bond yields

Market expectations of future inflation are an important determinant of long-term yields. If the financial markets expect a country's inflation rate to be persistently high, they will demand to be compensated in the form of comparably high interest rates. In this context, the experience of France and Germany in recent years is illuminating. France's commitment to its 'franc fort' policy, i.e. the policy during the 1980s of a strong French franc within the ERM of the EMS, has contributed to a steady reduction in expectations concerning future long-term inflation. In contrast, Germany's problems, following the unification of West and East Germany in the autumn of 1990, have produced intense cost and budgetary pressures, and have resulted in expectations of higher inflation over the next few years. The result has been a steady reduction in the difference between French and German long-term government bond yields, from 8% in 1982 to less than 0.5% at present. In other words, investors now believe that French and German inflation rates will in the long term be virtually identical.

Index-linking

An effective method of coping with some of the most destabilizing effects of high inflation is to establish a direct link between, on the one hand, the capital value of financial assets and, on the other hand, a whole range of contracts relating to incomes and changes in prices. The protection of purchasing power in this way is attractive for economic as well as for political reasons during periods of very rapid inflation, when the destabilizing effects of inflation and its adverse effects on large groups in society are most acute. By linking financial contracts and transactions (such as loans, deposits and other asset prices) as well as various incomes, including wages, to the rate of inflation (expressed, for example, by an index of retail prices), many of the arbitrary results of inflation can be mitigated. This technique of index-linking has been used in many countries (including Argentina, Brazil and Israel) which have all experienced long periods of high inflation in recent decades, at times exceeding 100% per annum. Index-linking has also been used in European countries, notably Italy, where the 'scala mobile' system of wage indexation has been a feature of economic policy for many years.

While indexation undoubtedly helps alleviate some of the symptoms of inflation, it does little in itself to attack the root causes of the problem. It can even be argued that a widespread system of indexation 'institutionalizes' inflation, in that the greater protection there is against the effects of sustained price rises, the less the political pressure on the government to deal with the problem. However, if a government index-links its own debt it cannot use further inflation to reduce the debt burden, and this may give it a powerful financial incentive to tackle the problem.

In the early 1980s, inflation in the UK was running at well over 10% and the government considered the case for index-linking its debt instruments. A limited scheme had already been in existence since 1975, whereby certain National Savings Certificates were index-linked, but this was restricted to pensioners. Inflation-proof national savings through the Save-As-You-Earn Scheme was also in existence at the time. The government decided that, despite the obvious disadvantage of extending index-linking because of the potential cost entailed in servicing high-coupon long-dated gilts, it would on balance be right to issue index-linked gilts. Firstly, it was felt that the new index-linked instruments would give the Bank of England additional flexibility in its debt marketing operations, with an ability to match investor preferences for either conventional fixed-interest or index-linked gilts. This could be particularly useful at times of rising inflation, when indexed gilts would be more attractive, thus making it possible for the authorities to fund the Public Sector Borrowing Requirement (PSBR) without raising nominal interest rates. Secondly, investors acquiring indexed gilts would enjoy reduced uncertainty about future inflation, and might in return accept a lower real rate of interest, thus reducing the overall cost of servicing government debt. Index-linked gilts were introduced in March 1981, and six months later index-linked National Savings Certificates became available to everybody regardless of age, though with a permitted maximum holding which was raised over time and at the end of 1991 was £10 000 per individual.

While index-linked instruments are a fairly modest part (14%) of total outstanding UK government debt, they will remain a useful and probably permanent component in the UK debt market. It is interesting to note that index-linked gilts provide one of the few objective measures of *expected inflation*. Given that all government debt is of equal riskiness, one can obtain an *objective market view* of expected inflation, simply by subtracting the real return of an index-linked instrument from the gross nominal yield of a fixed interest government security of similar maturity. Figure 3.4 shows movements in expected inflation in the UK by this definition.

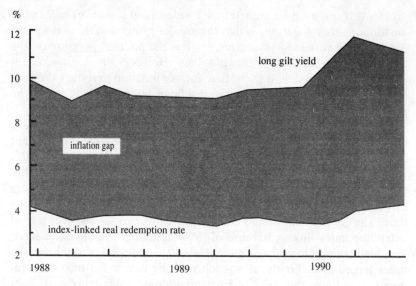

Figure 3.4 Expected inflation

Conclusion

Inflation is a fundamental issue which will appear frequently in the remainder of this book. This chapter has shown that the relationship between inflation and the general level of interest rates is crucial for the following reasons: (1) inflation is a key ingredient in the level of interest rates; (2) the policy response of governments to the management of the economy in general and the control of inflation in particular, involves changes in interest rates as one of the most important policy instruments; and (3) there are important links between a country's external financial position, the level of its exchange rate and its domestic inflation relative to other countries. If a country has a rate of inflation appreciably higher than that of its trading partners, its exports will become uncompetitive and imports from abroad will appear cheaper. The result will usually be a combination of lower exports and higher imports, with the current account of the balance of payments deteriorating and with growing pressures for the currency to devalue. The nature and scale of the official response will depend on the exchange rate regime in force – whether fixed or floating – as explained in Chapter 8. Whatever the system in operation, the role of interest rates is crucial. Finally, expectations of future inflation exert an important influence on long-term rates, an area which will be investigated in Chapter 4.

28

CHAPTER 4

The interest rate yield curve

The discussion in previous chapters has deliberately revolved around the concept of a single rate of interest. This is a helpful simplification when introducing a complex subject, but is clearly unrealistic. Rates of interest vary according to many factors including: the type of asset; the borrower's creditworthiness; the size of the transaction; the currency involved; and the term of the loan or asset. In this chapter, we drop the simplistic assumption about a single rate of interest, and focus on the different rates of interest available on identical assets with different times to maturity. In particular, reasons for the variation in interest rates of different maturity are assessed and the nature of the relationship between short-and longer-term rates examined.

In the discussion which follows, the term 'interest rate' is used synonymously with the term 'yield'; or, more precisely, the 'redemption yield' available from an asset. Whenever one deals with assets whose capital value remains unchanged throughout their lifetime, interest rates and yields are clearly synonymous. However, since the capital value of a marketable asset does change over time, the yield must be considered as including not only the interest receipts or payments on the asset, but also any capital appreciation/depreciation at the time of maturity arising from changes over time in the market value of the asset, expressed as a yearly percentage. Using interest rate and yield to mean virtually the same thing (i.e. the rate of return per annum) is entirely logical, once it is accepted that financial instruments are purchased on the understanding that either the existing holder or some subsequent owner buying the asset in the market place will be holding it until maturity.

The yield curve

Because a variety of factors affect interest rates, it is useful to be able to isolate the specific effects on interest rates of the maturity of the asset element. This is done by comparing the spread of interest rates over time paid on the *same type of security*. For the purpose of such a comparison, it is customary to use government debt instruments. These are free of default risk and thus can exhibit clearly the essential relationship between yields on different maturities. In addition, it is customary to use rates on inter-bank deposits, which are traded commercially in the money market, to construct yield curves, or term structures, for interest rates up to 12 months. The spread of rates across different maturities is usually represented diagrammatically by plotting the yields or interest rates on different maturities of debt over a number of time periods. The resulting yield curve shows the term structure of rates at a particular date; and examining changes in the yield curve over time provides useful information about monetary policy and about expectations. Figures 4.1–4.3 illustrate this concept.

The yield curve shown in Figure 4.1 has a 'normal' upward sloping shape. It indicates a gradual rise in interest rates as the maturity lengthens, then flattens out at the long end of the maturity spectrum as yields on very long-dated stocks tend to be close to each other. To be precise, a 'normal' yield curve is defined as one where the sole reasons for the rising slope relate to risk and liquidity and, therefore the implicit expectation is that rates will remain unchanged over time. Figure 4.2, where the upward slope is much steeper than in a 'normal' yield curve, implies expectations of rising rates. Conversely, Figure 4.3 shows a downward sloping yield curve, reflecting the unusual condition of short-term rates exceeding long-term rates. This indicates a situation where the market expects a pronounced fall in interest rates.

The different shapes of these yield curves, and their movements over time, have important implications for interest rate analysis and forecasting. In order to understand these implications, it is necessary to appreciate the forces which determine the shape of the yield curve at any time. These forces are in fact quite complex and there is considerable controversy over which factors best explain the shape of the term structure. The factors on which attention needs to be focused are:
1. risk and liquidity
2. expectations.

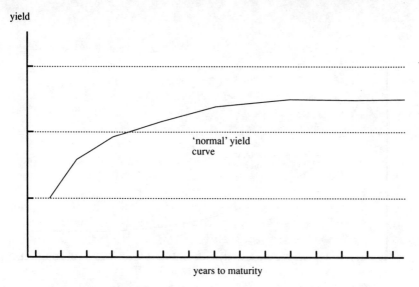

Figure 4.1 'Normal' yield curve

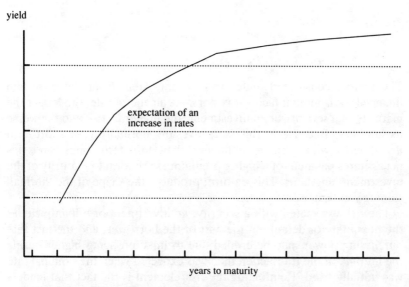

Figure 4.2 Expectation of an increase in rates

31

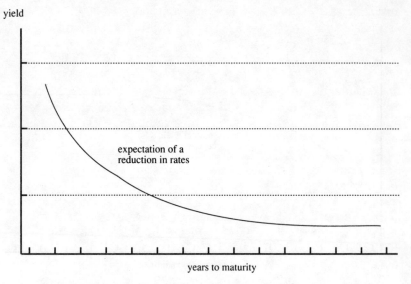

yield

expectation of a
reduction in rates

years to maturity

Figure 4.3 Expectation of a reduction in rates

Risk and liquidity factors

The factors considered under this heading stem from the uncertain financial environment facing investors. As a general rule, the longer the maturity of a security or an investment, the higher its risk and the worse its liquidity. Because of this fact, investors normally view short-term investments with greater confidence than long-term ones; and this necessitates payment of a higher premium as the term to maturity of the investment lengthens. This, in turn, produces the shape of the 'normal' sloping yield curve.

The risk associated with a security, an investment or a loan includes the possibility of default on the part of the borrower, and the fact that purchasing power may be eroded due to inflation being higher during the lifetime of the transaction than was expected when the nominal rate was initially fixed. Reinforcing the risk element is the fact that lenders require to be compensated for the loss of liquidity (or loss of access to immediate purchasing power) inherent in longer fixed-term loans. As with risk, the longer the term to maturity, the greater the interest premium required by the lender to compensate for loss of liquidity. The loss of liquidity occurs even if marketable debt is involved, since the risk of capital loss in the event of a premature sale implies a loss of liquidity.

Expectations theory

In explaining the term structure of interest rates, the theory focuses on expectations of future interest rate movements. The following assumptions are required to show the role of expectations: (1) in seeking to maximize profit, investors have no preference between holding a long-term security or a series of short-term securities (ignoring the transaction costs of shifting between short- and long-term securities); and (2) the long-term rate of interest is equal to the average of the current short-term rate plus the short-term rates of interest that the market expects during the lifetime of the long-term security.

The following example illustrates this, using the assumptions that (1) market participants have a choice between a 1-year and a 2-year bond; and (2) funds are available for use over the 2-year period.

Current rate of interest for 1-year bond:	10%
Expected rate of interest for 1-year bond 12 months from now:	15%
Actual rate of interest for 2-year bond:	12.47%

The rate for 2-year bonds is thus approximately the average of the current 1-year rate and the expected 1-year rate over the maturity of the bond, i.e.

$$\frac{10\% + 15\%}{2} = 12.5\%$$

While for practical purposes it is sufficient to approximate the result by averaging the two rates of interest, the precise calculation involves taking the geometric mean, calculated by using the square root since two years are involved, as shown below:

$$\sqrt{1.10 \times 1.15} = 1.1247$$

The rate of interest is then obtained by deducting 1 from 1.1247 and multiplying by 100. The crucial point in expectations theory is that, although individual traders may have different opinions about future trends, the net effect is a 'market view' about future short-term rates which, as in the example above, produces an actual current rate for

33

longer-term investments, irrespective of whether such expectations are in fact realized. The precise shape of the yield curve thus depends on the whole range of short-term rates expected to prevail at different times in the future. If the market expects short-term rates to increase, the yield curve will slope more sharply upwards than the 'normal' case, defined as a situation in which there are no expectations of interest rate changes and the yield curve's upward slope depends entirely on considerations of risk and liquidity. However, once there are expectations that interest rates will rise, the yield curve will become steeper than in the 'normal' case. Conversely, if market expectations are for short-term rates to decline in the future, the yield curve would be downward sloping. It should be stressed, however, that a yield curve which is entirely flat, or which is less steep than the 'normal' curve, also indicates expectations of modest declines in interest rates.

An analysis of the actions of lenders and borrowers (or savers and investors in the terminology of Chap. 1) helps to explain the impact of expectations on the term structure. If we assume, for example, that interest rates are expected to rise, *lenders* will seek to avoid being locked in at relatively low interest rates. They will therefore wish to lend only for very short terms in the expectation that, as loans mature, they will be able to re-lend at higher rates. Thus, there will tend to be an increase in the supply of funds for short-term investment, and a corresponding reduction in the supply of funds for longer-term lending. *Borrowers*, on the other hand will wish to borrow at the current lower rates for as long a maturity as possible so as to save on future interest costs. In doing so they increase demand for long-term funds, correspondingly reducing demand for short-term finance.

Observing changes in both the supply and demand for funds in a situation where interest rates are expected to rise, we see emerging at the short end of the market an excess of supply over demand, and at the long end excess demand in relation to supply. The effect will be that short-term interest rates will fall, while long-term rates rise; as explained earlier, the upward slope of the yield curve becomes steeper, as illustrated in Figure 4.2. The process will come to an end and equilibrium will be restored when the gap between long and short rates is regarded as sufficiently large to compensate for market expectations of a future rise in rates.

When there are expectations of a reduction in interest rates, the reactions of lenders and borrowers are the opposite of those described above. These reactions lead initially to excess demand for short-term funds and excess supply of long-term funds. The result will be a rise in short-term rates and a decline in long-term rates, producing a flatter yield curve than the 'normal' one. Indeed, a downward sloping curve, with short-term rates higher than long-term rates, could emerge if the falls in rates that the market is expecting are quite sharp.

The shape of the yield curve can be a useful guide to analysis and forecasting. Admittedly, considerable judgement has to be exercised, since the shape of a 'normal' term structure is not known for certain, and there can be variations in the 'normal' yield curve – both between countries and over time. In particular, a downward sloping yield curve has been more common in the UK than in either the US or Western Europe. Nevertheless, useful conclusions can often be drawn. For example, towards the end of 1990, both the UK and the US had downward sloping yield curves, indicating that the markets had strong expectations at that time of a reduction in interest rates. The strength of the expectation and the size of the reduction expected were sufficient to outweigh the influence of the risk and liquidity preference factors which tend to produce the normal upward-sloping curve.

In addition to its frequent downward sloping shape the UK's yield curve often has a pronounced 'hump' which occurs at maturities of between 5 and 10 years. This peculiarity may partially reflect expectations of rising interest rates in the late 1990s, but is mainly due to the maturity distribution of gilt-edged stock in the market (Fig. 4.4). Some £40 billion worth of stocks out of a total of £125 billion mature between 1995 and 2001, reflecting the very high funding requirements of the UK government during the 1970s and early 1980s. This volume of supply has

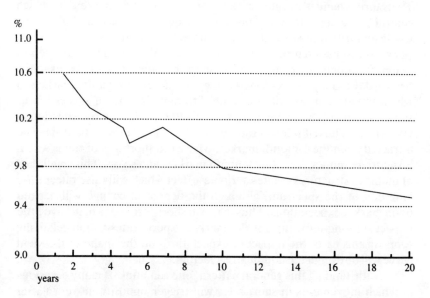

Figure 4.4 UK yield curve, March 1992

35

the effect of depressing gilt prices for these maturities, increasing yields at this part of the yield curve.

Relationship between short- and long-term rates

The spread of interest rates across the maturity spectrum, depicted in the yield curve, represents a continuum of rates from the short to the long end. However, one should draw a fundamental distinction between the basic factors determining both levels and changes in interest rates at either end of the spectrum. Very short-term rates are usually dominated by central bank operations in the money market, which are undertaken with the aim of avoiding volatility, but are largely determined by the requirements of monetary policy. Long-term rates are mainly influenced by market forces, crucially such factors as the government's funding requirements, private sector net demand for long-term funds and, perhaps most significantly, expectations about the future rate of inflation. However, there is a strong connection between short-term rates and longer-term rates which is implicit in the yield curve and is evidenced in practice by the fact that a large change in rates at the short end (as a result of government action) will usually be associated with a smaller change in the same direction in long-term rates. This effect arises because the markets in which dealings take place are competing and connected. Therefore, changes in rates in the short-term money markets, in which central banks are often key players, are quickly transmitted along the whole maturity time scale to the long end of the gilts market.

This transmission process does not require holders of financial assets to switch from one end of the time scale to the opposite end, for example from 7-day money to very long-term gilts. These are separate markets in which investment criteria are quite different. Rather, a succession of small movements along the time-scale is sufficient for the transmission to take effect. Thus, if interest rates in the 7-day market rise, funds may be attracted from the 1-month market, where the shortages of funds will in turn attract money from the 3-month market, and so on. This small shift of maturity structures creates a 'ripple' effect which will raise rates at the long end of the spectrum, although the degree of change will depend upon market expectations. Thus, a rise in short-term rates may have little impact on long-term rates if the market expects rates to fall relatively soon. In this case, the impact of expectations on the shape of the yield curve will outweigh the liquidity/risk factors.

Notwithstanding this general pattern, one can think of many occasions in which movements in short rates will trigger opposite moves in long rates. This will occur when the change in short rates generates a change in inflationary expectations. For example, if an increase in short rates is perceived as a firm anti-inflation move, long rates could ease with the yield curve flattening. Conversely, if a cut in short rates is seen as exacerbating future inflation, the result could be a rise in long rates and a steepening in the yield curve.

Changes in the yield curve over the economic cycle

The above analysis has shown that the shape of the yield curve at any point in time is effectively determined by the influence of expectations, which can be sufficiently strong to reverse or accentuate the 'normal' slope of the curve, as determined by liquidity and risk considerations. Thus, different expectations about the future course of interest rates, such as occur at different points in the economic cycle, are likely to have a strong influence on the shape of the yield curve.

Moreover, since yield curve analysis relates to nominal rates of interest, changes in the actual or expected rate of inflation will not only affect the shape of the yield curve, but also its position. For example, if inflation is relatively high, the yield curve of nominal rates will be located higher up the vertical axis than at a time when inflation is much lower. If it is expected that future inflation will be reduced considerably, then this will imply corresponding reductions in long-term nominal rates, causing the yield curve to flatten or even slope downward.

Figures 4.5 and 4.6 illustrate these points about the shape and position of the yield curve at different phases of the economic cycle. During a period of rising inflation in the UK in the late 1980s, nominal interest rates rose, exacerbated by rising inflationary pressure and the expectation that real interest rates would also have to increase as a policy response to the threat of higher inflation. The figures show clearly the impact on the position of the yield curve in successive years, as a result of progressively higher inflation and higher real interest rates. The impact of expectations on the slope of the curve is also illustrated – the slopes change from 'normal' in 1987 to sharply downward-sloping in 1989, reflecting strong expectations of interest rate reductions in the latter year.

The yield curves for the US over the same three years show a broadly similar picture, with rising inflation and interest rates (see Table 4.1) moving the yield curve higher up the vertical axis, but with the shape of the curve changing radically in 1989. It is interesting to note that in 1989 expectations beyond five years were for lower rates than expectations revealed by the 1988 yield curve.

37

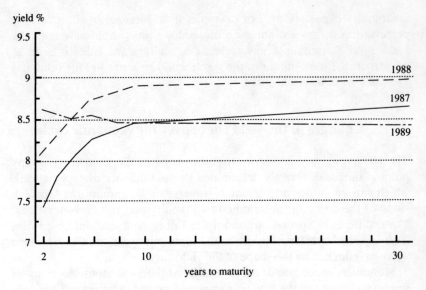

Figure 4.5 US yield curves, 1987–89

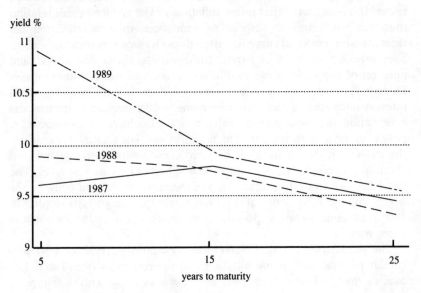

Figure 4.6 UK yield curves, 1987–89

38

Table 4.1   UK and US inflation and average interest rates

%	1987	1988	1989
UK			
Inflation	4.1	4.9	7.8
Interest rates*	9.4	9.9	13.4
US			
Inflation	3.7	4.1	4.8
Interest rates*	5.9	6.9	8.4

*3-month Treasury Bills

Conclusion

This chapter has shown that the concept of the yield curve occupies an important place in the analysis and forecasting of interest rates. By considering the shape of the yield curve and by investigating the factors which produce that shape, useful information can be gleaned about the forces operating at both ends of the maturity spectrum. Additionally, and most importantly, however, the shape of the yield curve'in relation to the 'normal' curve provides an indication of the collective or market view about short-term interest rates. As we have seen, expectations of interest rate movements exert an influence – sometimes a dominant influence – on the yield curve, over-riding fundamental risk and liquidity considerations. How good the yield curve is as a predictor of interest rates, compared with the forecasting approaches discussed later in this book, is debatable.

CHAPTER 5

Interest rates and risk

The pattern of interest rates is complex because each borrowing and lending transaction encompasses a variety of characteristics. Consideration of the yield curve in the previous chapter highlighted two crucial elements in this context: (1) the time to maturity of a financial asset; and (2) expectations. Two additional key factors which account for the wide variety of rates of interest in the financial system are: (3) the availability of different rates for different currencies, the subject of Chapter 8, and (4) the risk element and the way it is reflected through interest rates.

In general, the rate of interest must take into account the creditworthiness of the debtor. The lender always faces the risk of nonpayment by the borrower and the interest rate payable thus carries a 'loading' element which reflects this. For the borrower there is a risk that the lender is allowed repayment on demand for certain types of lendings such as overdrafts. Repayment at short notice at a time of economic presure could put the entire business at risk and lenders may be prepared to accept a lower interest rate if they have this option. This chapter examines the relationship between various aspects of the risk element and interest rates – mainly from the point of view of the lender.

Interest rate differences on various types of asset

The lowest risk of default is associated with central government debt, which for all practical purposes is effectively considered to be risk-free. Carrying slightly greater risk and a higher rate of interest are debt instruments issued by local authorities and first class companies. This is most easily illustrated at the short end of the market, because comparisons at the long end are often distorted by the complexities involved in

40

Table 5.1 Different rates available

	London		New York	
	1-month	3-months	1-month	3-months
Central government (Treasury Bills)	10.25	10.00	5.10	4.96
Local authority deposits	10.50	10.50	n.a.	n.a.
Commercial bills	10.81	10.63	5.23	5.30

calculating gross yields on gilts and equities. A typical pattern of rates in the London and New York money markets is shown in Table 5.1, which compares the different rates available on central and local government instruments, and on first class corporate paper.

The corporate sector is represented in Table 5.1 by a single interest rate on commercial bills for each time period and financial centre. This simplification ignores the fact that there is a wide range of corporate risk, depending on the relative financial strength of each company, and that the interest rates quoted in the market will vary accordingly. Even for paper issued by the same company, the rate of interest will vary according to the perceived risk attached to different forms of borrowing. This can be seen by considering the interest payable on different categories of debt which may be defined in broad terms, according to their relative legal standing, as senior debt, mezzanine debt and equities. Senior debt carries the lowest 'loading' for risk, reflecting its stronger position against other forms of debt in the event of liquidation. Senior debt has a priority status over mezzanine debt in such circumstances; while mezzanine debt, in turn, must be paid before equity holders' claims can be satisfied by the value realized through the residual value of the business, if any.

The role of the rating agencies

Investors purchasing bonds or commercial paper require an independent assessment of the creditworthiness of the borrower. For their part, the bond issuers (i.e. the borrowers) can also benefit from having their debt rated, in that an objective rating can assist market recognition and is indeed an essential requirement in the US for some forms of borrowing. Issuers, therefore, frequently initiate the rating process. In the US, credit rating of corporate and municipal bonds has been well established for several decades. Since the late 1960s, a credit rating has also been assigned to commercial paper. The two main credit-rating

41

institutions – Moody's and Standard & Poor's – are both based in New York and have offices in major financial centres worldwide. Each provides a credit rating to the securities of several thousand corporate and municipal issuers. Credit rating in Europe is less developed than in the US, but demand is growing and it is becoming increasingly important for issuers to have a rating to ensure demand for commercial paper and bond issues.

The rating companies adopt a broadly similar approach in assessing corporate paper, carrying out detailed analysis of the company, its products and its markets. The analysis is fairly mechanistic and largely focuses on a number of standard financial ratios related to the company's debt burden. Consideration is also made of broad financial factors such as the company's track record over a period of years, its earnings and its future balance sheet performance. Non-financial factors are also covered by assessing the prospects for the industry in which the company operates, and the company's competitive position. Management is evaluated in terms of its operational success, plans, policies and overall quality. In the commercial paper analysis, emphasis is also placed on liquidity considerations.

For investors, the conclusions reached by the rating agencies provide an important part of the decision-making process. For borrowers, a satisfactory rating is often an essential pre-condition for raising funds and the grade awarded can be a key determinant of the interest rate the company will have to pay. If a particular security is traded in the secondary market, the rating is one of the key factors determining its price and its interest yield relative to the market as a whole. The Standard & Poor's grades for long-term investments are shown below.

Standard & Poor's rating definitions

Long-term investment grades

AAA The highest degree of safety with overwhelming repayment capacity.

AA Very high degree of safety with very strong capacity for repayment. These issues differ from higher rated issues only in a small degree.

A A strong degree of safety and capacity for repayments, but these issues are somewhat more susceptible in the long term to adverse economic conditions than those rated in higher categories.

BBB A satisfactory degree of safety and capacity for repayment, but these issues are more vulnerable to adverse economic conditions or changing circumstances than higher rated issues.

Long-term speculative grades

CDs (Certificates of Deposit) rated in these categories have predominantly speculative characteristics in their ability to repay interest and principal. BB indicates the lowest degree of speculation and C the highest.

BB   This designation reflects less near-term vulnerability to default than other speculative issues. However, the issues face major on-going uncertainties or exposures to adverse economic or financial conditions threatening capacity to meet interest and principal payments on a timely basis.

B   This designation indicates that the issues have a greater vulnerability to default but currently have the capacity to meet interest payments and principal repayments. Adverse business, financial or economic conditions will likely impair capacity to pay interest and repay principal.

CCC   Issues rated CCC have currently identifiable vulnerability to default and are dependent upon favourable business, financial and economic conditions to meet timely interest and principal repayments. Adverse business, financial or economic developments would render repayment capacity unlikely.

Interest rates payable by sovereign borrowers are also dependent on risk perceptions. Many large international banks and other major corporates have internal country risk assessment systems to evaluate the degree of risk involved in lending to, or doing business with, individual countries. Such systems use a mixture of financial indicators (such as external debt in relation to GNP and debt-service ratios) and political factors to assess the degree of risk associated with each country. In some circumstances, when the businesses being evaluated carry very different risk criteria, banks and other lenders find it appropriate to use a number of risk rankings simultaneously – for example, one for short-term trade finance and one for medium-term loans. This practice is similar to an agency giving the same borrower different ratings for bonds and for commercial paper.

Conclusion

Although this book focuses mainly on the factors to be considered in forecasting the general level of interest rates, it is important to appreciate

43

the key determinants of maturity and risk which account for the existence of a wide range of rates around the notional 'general level'. It is also important to appreciate that the general or average level of interest rates cannot be entirely separated either from the maturity structure or from the degree of risk involved. For example, changes in the risk perception relating to the financial system as a whole will affect expectations, and through them the average level of rates as well as the maturity structure.

CHAPTER 6

Monetary policy

In Chapter 1, brief reference was made to the powerful impact of government actions on short-term interest rates. This chapter and the following one examine *why* and *how* this influence is exercised. The focus in this chapter is on why governments find it necessary to manipulate interest rates. This will involve a consideration of monetary policy – its role, objectives and the instruments used in seeking to achieve those objectives – as an introduction to the implementation of policy and its direct consequences for interest rates, which form the basis of the next chapter.

The role of monetary policy

Governments in all countries have several key economic objectives, including satisfactory growth in the economy, the control of inflation, the achievement of high employment levels and balancing the external accounts. Other possible aims can relate to desired changes in the country's regional or industrial structure. Monetary policy is only one of a package of policies available to governments to fulfil these objectives, but for most major economies it is probably the most important element. The other policy tools in this package are fiscal policy and direct controls over specific aspects of the economy: for example, over prices and incomes, and foreign exchange movements.

The balance between the different policy tools available changes in line with the political and ideological preferences of different governments, and the intellectual fashion prevailing at different times. Most governments have avoided a doctrinaire approach and have normally taken a pragmatic view, using a wide range of policy techniques. Even so, there have been periods in recent decades when one form or other of

45

policy has been predominant. In the first 25–30 years after the end of the Second World War, fiscal policy, i.e. changes in public spending and in taxation, was the dominant policy tool; but in the late 1970s and early 1980s monetary policy assumed a prominent role in both the US and the UK. The importance attached to monetary policy at that time reflected the weight given in the formulation of policy to the school described as 'monetarist', where strict control of money supply growth is seen as being paramount in influencing other economic variables, notably the rate of inflation. In more recent years, although monetary policy has retained its dominant position as the main technique for controlling the economy, rigid monetarism has given way to a more flexible approach in which a wider range of indicators has been given weight in the formulation of policy, particularly the exchange rate and the level of real interest rates.

Monetary policy in practice: the UK and the US

In the UK, money supply control emerged as an increasingly dominant feature of economic policy during the 1970s, as the objective of policy in general became focused on the priority of reducing the rate of inflation. In 1976, the authorities introduced for the first time the practice of setting targets for growth in certain chosen monetary aggregates. This was based on the belief that there was a reasonably stable and close relationship between the behaviour of these money aggregates and, after a lag of some 18–24 months, the growth in total spending in the economy and ultimately the inflation rate. In order to provide a degree of flexibility, these money supply targets were expressed in terms of broad ranges, which were to be reduced gradually in successive years, with the intention of influencing private sector expectations about inflation by showing that the authorities meant business about controlling the money supply and hence inflation.

The results of this approach were disappointing. During the 1980s, money supply targets were consistently exceeded by a wide margin. This was partly due to special factors, such as the liberalization of financial markets which occurred during the period, and the prevailing high level of real interest rates, both of which distorted money supply figures. At the same time, the inherent difficulties in controlling the money stock, given the conflicting demands of other objectives, constrained the effective operation of policy. For example, the level of interest rates required to meet a target for the growth of the money stock may well be different from that required to keep the exchange rate at a particular level, and these at times conflicting influences contributed to the difficulties of controlling money supply growth. The targets set, and the actual outturns for the 1980s, are shown in Table 6.1

In addition to these practical difficulties, there were some fundamental intellectual problems associated with this policy approach. Firstly, there was considerable uncertainty as to what aggregate should be controlled. Targeting more than one aggregate often gave conflicting messages. Secondly, the authorities were on occasion genuinely uncertain as to how a particular target should be achieved. Thirdly, and most importantly, the relationship between money supply growth and inflation proved to be more variable and more ambiguous than was envisaged by 'simplistic monetarism'. Thus, despite the erratic behaviour of the broad money aggregates in the mid-1980s, there was not an immediate upsurge in inflation. Indeed, the inflation rate declined steadily to below 4% in 1986 at a time when money supply growth appeared to be rapid. In recognition of the fact that the behaviour of broad money aggregates had not been a good guide to the course of inflation, the targeting of these indicators was abandoned in the 1987/88

Table 6.1   UK monetary targets, 1980–92

Target set	Target period	Monetary target	Target growth range (%) p.a.	Actual outcome (% p.a.)
Mar 1980	Feb 1980/Apr 1981	£M3	7–11	18.5
Mar 1981	Feb 1981/Apr 1982	£M3	6–10	14.5
Mar 1982	Feb 1982/Apr 1983	M1	8–12	14.3
		£M3	8–12	11.1
		PSL2	8–12	11.3
Mar 1982	Feb 1983/Apr 1984	M1	7–11	14.0
		£M3	7–11	9.4
		PSL2	7–11	13.1
Mar 1984	Feb 1984/Apr 1985	M0	4–8	5.5
		£M3	6–10	11.6
Mar 1985	Apr 1985/Apr 1986	M0	3–7	3.3
		£M3	5–9	16.5
Mar 1986	Apr 1986/Apr 1987	M0	2–6	5.2
		£M3	11–15	20.5
Mar 1987	Apr 1987/Apr 1988	M0	2–6	6.4
Mar 1988	Apr 1988/Apr 1989	M0	1–5	6.2
Mar 1989	Apr 1989/Apr 1990	M0	1–5	7.2
Mar 1990	Apr 1990/Apr 1991	M0	1–5	1.2
Mar 1991	Apr 1991/Apr 1992	M0	0–4	

Source: Bank of England Quarterly Bulletin, various issues
Notes: £M3 and PSL 2 were renamed in May 1987 as M3 and M5 respectively

budget. However, as had been predicted by some analysts, the growth of broad money aggregates in the mid-1980s was followed by a resurgence of inflation in the later years of the decade.

A narrow measure of money (M0) has continued to be targeted, as shown in Table 6.1, but the focus of monetary policy in the UK has shifted from money supply targets to the exchange rate. For much of 1987 and 1988, the pound shadowed the Deutschmark informally, and this relationship became formalized when, in October 1990, it was announced that sterling would enter the Exchange Rate Mechanism (ERM) of the European Monetary System (EMS). The discipline imposed by the commitment to keep sterling within its agreed band against other ERM currencies has become the over-riding influence on UK interest rates, and the most important anchor of the government's anti-inflation policy.

In the US, the introduction of a policy involving the setting and announcing of formal targets for monetary growth occurred in 1975, slightly earlier than in the UK. However, as was the case in the UK, experience fell short of expectation. There was an initial success, with very tight monetary policies contributing to a reduction in inflation, from 13.5% in 1980 to 3.2% in 1983. However, given the long and variable lags involved in economic relationships, it became increasingly difficult to assess the implications of monetary growth for the future rate of inflation. Consequently, fluctuations in the monetary aggregates proved less reliable guides than expected as to when, and by how much, interest rates needed to adjust to monetary developments. Strict adherence to monetarist principles has been replaced by a more pragmatic approach. This involves a consideration of developments in the real economy, taking into account factors such as consumer and business confidence, investment intentions and economic growth.

While this pragmatism gives policy makers in the UK and the US greater flexibility and avoids the straightjacket of rigid monetarism, it also contains many risks. For example, there might have been good reasons at the time for ignoring the fast monetary growth that occurred in the aftermath of the financial liberalization seen in the second half of the 1980s. With hindsight, however, it is clear that in the UK the relaxed approach to the upsurge in money and credit contributed to the 'Lawson boom' and the upturn in inflation. Monetary policy, in terms of the desired level of interest rates, is now aligned to trends in the real economy as well as to financial factors, particularly the foreign exchange markets and the relative strength or weakness of the country's financial institutions.

The stages of monetary policy

In the previous section, reference was made to two aspects of monetary policy – ultimate objectives (such as control of inflation) and instruments (such as interest rates). It would be useful at this stage to place these elements in a coherent framework so that the relationship between the various stages of monetary policy can be clearly seen. The following list shows these different stages:

ultimate objectives
    control of inflation and the creation of conditions to achieve economic growth, high employment levels and external balance
    exchange rate under an ERM type regime
intermediate targets
    money supply
    credit
    exchange rate
    interest rates
    liquid assets of banks
instruments
    interest rates
    open market operations
    portfolio constraints on banks
    direct controls. e.g. ceilings on lending.

Note that the exchange rate, although normally an intermediate target, also becomes an explicit 'ultimate objective' under an ERM-type regime. Also interest rates, although normally an instrument, can also be an operating or intermediate target.

Monetary policy is implemented through a series of links between these stages. The final stage is the ultimate goal of macroeconomic policy; the intermediate targets are economic variables through which the authorities attempt to realize these objectives, and instruments are variables over which the authorities are able to exert some direct control in seeking to influence intermediate targets.

It will be clear that the further up the list one moves, the weaker becomes the direct influence of the authorities. Close control can be exerted over instruments, but the impact on intermediate targets is much less effective. In attempting to influence the money supply (an intermediate target), for example, the authorities cannot predict or exercise complete control over the behaviour of banks and their customers; while the link between intermediate targets and expenditure is equally uncertain, being dependent on the public's spending behaviour.

The fact that, as mentioned already, the level of interest rates appears not only as an instrument of policy, but is also included as an intermediate target, requires some explanation: as an *instrument of policy*, interest rates are set directly by the authorities. This does not apply to all interest rates. As we have seen, the action of the authorities is only one determinant of interest rate levels. However, the rate at which the central bank is prepared to lend to the banking system when the market as a whole is short of funds is a crucial determinant of short-term rates. This key rate, known as the discount rate or intervention rate, has a pervasive influence on all other short-term rates and can be used by authorities, as explained in the following chapter.

As an *intermediate target*, the level of short-term rates is the level desired by the authorities as part of their monetary policy. It is produced by using the highly effective instrument of open market operations, as discussed in Chapter 7, to create or alleviate shortages in the money markets. In engaging in such operations, the authorities also wish to influence consumer or business activities and, therefore, the level of demand in the economy.

These aspects of the role of interest rates are important in understanding the operation of monetary policy. As we have seen, during the 1970s there was a marked shift in the focus of policy both in the US and the UK toward tight control of the money supply. As can be seen from the above explanation, this implied that interest rates were then being used as an operating target or an instrument. They could no longer be used as an intermediate target, since the authorities cannot simultaneously target both the money supply and the level of interest rates. If they target a particular rate of money supply growth, they have to accept whatever rate of interest is required. More recently, in the UK, the departure from strict monetarist principles involving close control over money supply growth, coupled with the depressed state of industry in the 1990/92 recession, have placed renewed emphasis on interest rates as an intermediate target. However, the authorities' ability to meet that target is counterbalanced by the need for interest rates to act as an instrument of policy in determining the exchange rate.

Conclusion

It should be apparent from this chapter that the role and application of monetary policy are highly relevant factors underlying interest rate movements. Whichever of the intermediate targets the authorities are aiming to control, the leverage exercised by the various instruments available will automatically affect or involve the use of interest rates. In the next chapter, we examine how the authorities exercise this influence.

CHAPTER 7

The role of central banks

As the issue and the management of a country's currency constitutes a vital attribute of national sovereignty and an important element of overall economic policy, responsibility for the formulation and implementation of monetary policy normally lies solely with governments. However, in some countries central banks are constitutionally provided with a degree of autonomy which gives them considerable independence in decision-making, and it is sometimes argued that this absence of political control gives more responsible and effective monetary policies. While this chapter is mainly concerned with the implementation of policy, we begin by examining briefly the issue of central bank independence, which is not only of intrinsic importance but can also have an effect in some circumstances on the level of interest rates.

Central bank independence

Responsibility for most aspects relating to the execution of monetary policy is delegated to central banks, although the extent of the powers delegated varies considerably among countries. Central banks are almost universally responsible for the day-to-day operation of policy. However, in some countries (such as Germany and the US), the central bank, being constitutionally independent from the government, is also empowered to determine a number of key policy features. In other countries, including the UK, France and Japan, the government has the full legal responsibility for the conduct of monetary policy. In practice, the differences are less pronounced than is sometimes claimed. Independent central banks cannot ignore political realities while, conversely, central banks that are legally subservient retain a large degree of influence over policy making. In any case, disagreement between the central bank and the government only rarely becomes public, given the damaging effect this could have on market confidence.

The whole issue of central bank independence is assuming greater prominence in Europe as the EC moves towards monetary union, and consideration is being given to the establishment of a federal central bank for the entire Community. There is strong pressure for this institution to be independent of politicians, who are often influenced by electoral considerations. In general, it is felt that the central bank's responsibility for keeping inflation under control could be carried out more effectively if such political interference were not legally permissible.

There are a number of issues to consider. One concerns the ultimate control of an independent central bank, i.e. its accountability for its actions and policy and whether, for example, accountability to parliament would satisfy the requirements of democratic control. This issue is of constitutional rather than economic importance, and need not concern us unduly, though the matter may assume greater significance within the EC where the future division of power between national parliaments and the European parliament is still unclear.

Another crucial question is whether central bank autonomy results in more effective control of inflation. There is no clear answer to this. There can be little doubt, for example, that on many occasions (not only in the run-up to general elections), governments in the UK have eased monetary policy and taken risks with inflation, while the independent Bundesbank has always given top priority to controlling inflation, and that the UK's record on inflation is undoubtedly inferior to that of Germany. Yet this contrast does not point us conclusively in favour of independent central banking. As Table 7.1 shows, independence is not in itself a sufficient condition to guarantee success. The independent US Federal Reserve Board (Fed) has had only a moderate record in controlling inflation and, for various reasons, has often reduced interest rates before Presidential elections. Also the Bank of Japan, which is

Table 7.1   The inflation record of various countries

Country	Central bank	Inflation record (1980–89 % per annum)
France	Subordinate	7.3
Japan	to government	2.5
UK	ministry	7.4
Germany	Independent	2.9
US		5.5

firmly under political control, has an excellent record in keeping inflation low. Furthermore, even in Germany, the Bundesbank is not always able to prevent the Federal Government from taking decisions which it regards as inflationary – for example, on the terms of unification between East and West Germany.

The above discussion regarding the powers of independent as opposed to subordinate central banks may have given the impression that the Bank of England has less influence than is in fact the case. Even though the Bank is ultimately obliged to carry out the government's policy decisions rather than its own, it is still a very influential institution. The Governor is more than just a functionary. He is allowed to express his views publicly and forcefully on policy issues, and the implied threat of his resignation over a vital policy matter could be a sufficiently powerful weapon to dissuade politicians from pursuing totally irresponsible monetary policies.

As mentioned already, the issue of independent central banking in the EC is particularly topical, in view of the steady move towards full economic and monetary union (EMU). While it can be reasonably argued that it is not acceptable for unelected officials, unaccountable for their actions, to have the power to make decisions with major economic and political implications, the issue of accountability is often exaggerated and can be resolved fairly easily. More serious, in practice, are the damaging problems that can arise when elected governments are allowed to put short-term electoral considerations above sound long-term economic policies. The obvious way to resolve any potential problem is to ensure that unelected officials of an independent central bank are appointed (or confirmed in office) by a democratically elected body, such as Parliament or the government, and have some form of statutory accountability to that elected body. In both the US and Germany, the respective constitutions provide for operational central bank independence and ultimate democratic control. Indeed, one could take accountability one stage further. Thus, the independent central bank could be set clear objectives for price stability by the elected Parliament and these objectives could be reviewed in the light of changing circumstances. The central bank would then be made accountable to Parliament both for the attainment of its detailed objectives and for the formulation of strategy. An experiment along these lines is now being undertaken in New Zealand, but it will take a few years to evaluate the results.

In practice, most of the fears concerning the consequences of giving too much power to central banks seem unfounded when one considers the actual experience of the two institutions with the greatest degree of independence – the US Fed and the German Bundesbank. It is also important to bear in mind that even the most autonomous central bank cannot over-ride the wishes of a determined government. For example, the Bundesbank, despite its constitutional remit to protect the value of the currency, had to face the embarrassing reality that its clear wishes over the precise financial terms of German unification were ignored by the West German government. Similarly, partly influenced by political considerations, the US Fed has at times felt obliged to cut interest rates, even though it disagreed with major aspects of policy, particularly the budget deficit. Even independent central banks cannot entirely disregard political considerations; however, they have a better chance on balance to resist such pressures.

Implementation of policy

As we have seen, central banks, whether independent or subordinate, have operational responsibility for implementing policy. The previous chapter highlighted the important role of interest rates, either as an operating policy target or as a policy instrument. To understand precisely how central banks influence interest rates in the direction required by monetary policy, it is necessary to appreciate the nature and scope of their operations in the domestic money and securities markets.

Open market operations

The money market

In most countries, the money markets are a key part of the financial system. The main transactions undertaken involve borrowing and lending short-term wholesale funds and the trading of short-term securities. There are a number of individual markets – e.g. interbank, local authority paper, Treasury Bills, Certificates of Deposits (CDs) – serving the requirements of specific groups of users, but the nature of these flexible markets makes for a highly integrated structure, with funds flowing easily between markets. The importance of the money markets in the context of central bank operations in influencing interest rates stems from two factors. Firstly, financial institutions use the markets to manage their day-to-day liquidity positions by holding in the money market their short-term deposits, and taking funds from the markets when they have net liquidity shortfalls. This pattern ensures that any change in interest rates as a result of central bank actions in the markets will be quickly reflected in the marginal cost of funds and, after a short lag, in commercial bank lending rates. Secondly, the money markets experience the full effect of the very large flows which take place each day as a result of transactions between the private sector and the government. The supply of cash in the markets can be materially altered as a result of net inflows or outflows arising from public sector expenditure transactions (for example, pensions and social security payments) and receipts (such as taxes and cheques received from sales of government securities). While government transactions can have a significant effect on the supply of cash in the money markets on a daily basis, over the financial year as a whole they have little net effect as long as the government broadly adheres to the practice of nil net funding – i.e., where the government neither overfunds nor underfunds its deficits and surpluses over the financial year. Nevertheless, the short-term mismatches in flows which occur enable central banks to play a crucial role in the markets. This role is exerted through open market operations – purchases and sales of various instruments such as government securities or eligible commercial bills – to influence conditions in the markets.

Depending on money market conditions and policy requirements at any particular time, a central bank will intervene in the markets to do one of the following:

- avoid volatility in the demand/supply balance for funds, and consequently prevent sharp fluctuations in interest rates
- ease or tighten monetary conditions in line with the cyclical position of the economy and the government's own policy aims.

If the aim is to *prevent volatility in interest rates*, the central bank will buy or sell securities to keep the supply and demand for funds in the market roughly in balance. In general, this is an important smoothing operation with only limited effect on the broader policy issues.

In order to *ease monetary conditions*, the central bank will engage in open market operations to over-compensate for any shortage, or refrain from fully offsetting a surplus, thus creating conditions to encourage a reduction in interest rates. Conversely, if the central bank is aiming to *tighten monetary conditions* (as a way of raising short-term interest rates), open market operations will be directed at creating a shortage of cash. This can be achieved either by selling more securities than are required to offset a surplus, or by not buying sufficient securities to offset a deficit fully.

The creation of a shortage aimed at exerting upward pressure on interest rates is not intended to create a situation in which the system as a whole will actually suffer an outright physical shortage of funds. The

55

central bank normally stands ready to act as 'lender of last resort', ensuring that the markets can obtain cash in the event of a shortage, though at a price determined by the central bank itself. In general, there are two ways of alleviating a shortage. The central bank can either rediscount, i.e. buy back securities from market institutions, or it can permit authorized institutions or banks to approach it for short-term facilities, again at a rate of its own choosing – either the official discount rate or a rate it gets for the bills it holds.

Long-term securities markets

We have already established that the monetary authorities' influence on interest rates is primarily at the short end of the maturity spectrum. At the longer end, interest rates are determined by market forces. However, central banks are normally also responsible for managing the government's outstanding debt portfolio and for issuing new debt. Such operations can have a strong impact on the demand/supply balance for long-term funds, thus exerting indirect pressure on interest rates at this part of the spectrum. Nevertheless, in most cases the authorities' influence on long-term rates is far less powerful and direct than their influence through money market operations on short-term rates.

Central bank money market operations in the US and the UK

Having examined the principles of central bank money market operations, we now consider briefly policy implementation in two countries, the US and the UK.

The central bank in the US – the Federal Reserve System or 'the Fed' – although ultimately responsible to the US Congress, is constitutionally independent from the President and the government's executive branch, and has therefore appreciable authority for policy making. This authority has become concentrated in the Federal Open Market Committee (FOMC), which was established to oversee the Fed's open market operations. Members of the FOMC include all seven governors of the system, the president of the New York Fed, and the presidents of four of the other eleven district (i.e. regional) banks which constitute the Federal Reserve System, who serve on a rotating basis.

The Fed's open market operations are directed by the FOMC, which meets regularly to review economic conditions and progress in achieving the guidelines or targets it has set for achieving monetary control. In moving short-term interest rates, to affect other policy objectives, the

Fed uses two methods. A powerful option, but one which is used infrequently, is to adjust the official rate at which institutions borrow from the Fed s discount window. This is applied when the Fed is acting in its capacity as lender of last resort, enabling institutions to make a short-term adjustment to their liquidity positions in times of market tightness. A change to the discount rate is a clear signal to the markets about the Fed's wishes and intentions. The more usual indicator of the Fed's short-term interest rate policy is the overnight Fed funds rate, the rate at which banks trade very short-term funds, movements in which are transmitted very rapidly to all other short-term rates. The Fed funds rate can be effectively dictated by the Fed's open market operations aimed at influencing conditions in the market. To tighten conditions, the Fed sells short-dated securities; while to relax conditions, it either buys securities or undertakes repos (repurchase agreements) with dealers in government securities.

In the UK, the Bank of England is responsible for implementing interest rate policy. This is ultimately determined by the Chancellor of the Exchequer as part of overall macroeconomic management, but the Bank of England usually has an important input in its formulation. Operationally, the Bank is able to influence short-term interest rates by virtue of its position as the government's main agent and operator in the money markets, mainly the London discount market which has traditionally constituted the core of money market arrangements in London. Despite many important changes in recent years, this market remains at the centre of the Bank of England's interest rate operations.

The discount market revolves around the activities of the discount houses, a small group of intermediary institutions which are a distinctive feature of the UK financial system. In other systems, central banks deal directly with commercial banks to influence market liquidity. The Bank of England in undertaking such operations deals largely with the discount houses, and only to a limited extent directly with commercial banks, although the techniques used – buying and selling bills (eligible commercial bills and Treasury Bills) and to a lesser extent sale and repurchase agreements – are basically the same as those in other countries.

The Bank of England's transactions are the result of its estimates of the likely size of any daily shortage or surplus in the market, announced to the money markets in the morning and, if necessary, revised at noon. Since the Bank is the ultimate source of liquidity in the market, its power to relieve any shortages also enables it to exert considerable influence on the desired level of very short-term interest rates. If there is a shortage (which can be deliberately engineered by the Bank), the Bank advises the discount houses that it is prepared to buy commercial or Treasury Bills from them, and the discount houses then offer bills at prices of their own choosing. If the interest rate implied by these prices is consistent with the authorities' view of the appropriate level of short-term rates, the Bank will accept the offers and the shortage will be relieved. However, if it is considered that the rates are too low, the Bank will decline to purchase bills, and the discount houses will be obliged to offer bills at lower prices. The authorities' action in raising short-term interest rates in this way is transmitted quickly throughout the system. When the Bank wishes to see a fall in rates, it simply increases the price at which it is prepared to buy bills from the discount houses. If the interest rate change desired and effected by the Bank of England is large enough (i.e. 0.5% or more), there will be a corresponding rise in commercial bank base rates as well as in other lending and deposit rates.

In operating the system outlined above, the authorities aim to keep short-term rates in an unpublished band set by the requirements of monetary policy. There is some flexibility within the band, and the band itself can be shifted without notifying the markets. The UK equivalent to the US discount rate was historically known as Bank Rate, or from 1971 to 1981 as Minimum Lending Rate. This official rate was abolished in 1981 in the belief that this would enable the authorities to act without the direct publicity that used to accompany changes in the official discount rate. In practice, however, interest rate changes made by the Bank of England still attract as much attention as ever because they are reflected almost instantaneously in changes in the general level of bank lending rates and, after some delay, also in mortgage interest rates which affect millions of people.

Conclusion

It is worth re-emphasizing in conclusion that the authorities' action in the money markets can very strongly *influence*, but not absolutely *control* the level of short-term rates. The authorities' powers are largely constrained by the markets' confidence in their commitment to basic policy aims such as the control of inflation or a stable exchange rate within the ERM. The stage of the economic cycle and external factors can also be relevant. Market forces, which take these factors into account, can occasionally be sufficiently strong to modify or even negate the impact of central bank operations. An adverse market reaction to a change in short-term interest rates is most likely to be felt in the foreign exchange market, through a speculative attack on the currency. Nevertheless, as this and the previous chapter have shown, the authorities can, if they wish, exercise a substantial influence on short-term interest rates, and this is transmitted to longer maturities. Whatever the precise interest rates used by the authorities – either an official discount rate, or a market rate, such as the Fed funds rate in the US or various bill rates in the UK – these rates will act as a fulcrum for the entire interest rate structure in the country.

CHAPTER 8

The international dimension

In considering the factors which explain interest rate levels and move-ments we have looked so far at the theoretical background; at condi-tions in the domestic economy such as inflation and liquidity; and at the overall monetary stance of the government. All these aspects have largely been evaluated within the framework of a domestic economy. It is therefore now appropriate to complete the picture by considering the international dimension. This is a very crucial aspect in the determina-tion of short-term interest rates and it can, occasionally, over-ride domestic considerations.

Interest rates and currencies – the basic relationships

The international dimension has assumed great importance because the globalization of financial markets and the massive volume of interna-tional capital moving rapidly between financial centres has intensified the close relationship between interest rates and exchange rates. The basic factors determining interest rates movements – government policy, cyclical factors, inflation and demand/supply factors – all have an important international dimension. There is also a fundamental tech-nical or mechanistic link between interest and exchange rates which operates through the forward market. Thus, for example, if 3-month sterling rates are 2% higher than 3-month dollar rates then, by definition sterling is at a 2% forward discount against the dollar for a 3-month maturity, and conversely, the dollar is at a 2% premium. This relationship, however, although highly important for money market traders, does not in itself tell us whether sterling will in fact fall or the dollar will rise over the next three months.

Even when one moves beyond the technical relationship operating through the forward market, it is not easy to predict how the interest rate/exchange rate relationship will operate. For example, a weak currency can often be defended by raising domestic interest rates. At the same time, over the longer term, strong currencies generally command lower rates, because the capital gains enjoyed by investors in strong currencies should enable them to accept a lower yield. In the first case, the level of rates is driven by an official policy decision; in the second, more by market reaction and expectations. To follow the precise linkages, it is important to understand the type of exchange rate regime in operation, and the exchange rate goals of individual countries within the system. The next section looks at the various types of exchange rate regimes and examines the arrangements currently in force.

Exchange rate regimes

International trade and finance can operate under a wide range of different types of exchange rate regimes. The extreme forms, rigidly fixed exchange rates and perfectly floating rates, are somewhat theoretical, but the variety of exchange rate regimes actually experienced has been quite wide.

Under a fixed exchange rate regime, each currency is required to keep within a predetermined narrow band around a fixed parity with other currencies. This means that when a currency threatens to move outside its fixed band, the authorities are obliged to take action, either by intervening directly in the foreign exchange markets (for example by buying their currency if it is weak) or by making the necessary adjustment to domestic interest rates, or by a combination of both. Intervention in the markets, although occasionally powerful and effective, ultimately has only a temporary impact, given that the amount of foreign exchange reserves at the disposal of the authorities is limited. If a country's exchange rate is under pressure due to fundamental economic weakness, it is highly unlikely that central bank intervention on its own can defend the value of the currency. In practice, therefore, the onus for the corrective action falls on more basic intervention through interest rate adjustment and other policy measures – for example, cutting public spending.

In a 'clean' floating exchange rate regime, the market's demand for, and supply of, currencies are allowed to determine exchange rates; deliberate official intervention, either direct or indirect, does not take place. In such a system, therefore, interest rates have no overt role, because there is no official exchange rate target. However, domestic-driven policies, for example, a rise in interest rates aimed at curtailing inflation, will have a powerful impact on the country's currency.

The Western trading nations have rarely operated a system of pure floating rates. This is because the exchange rate has important implications for key economic variables, notably export and import volumes, and the rate of inflation. Governments have, therefore, been reluctant to allow market forces to be the sole determinants of their currency's exchange value and they have in practice operated either a fixed exchange rate regime, or a 'managed' floating system, containing elements of both fixed and floating regimes. Such a hybrid system has been in force since the early 1970s, following the breakdown of the Bretton Woods regime of relatively fixed exchange rates (modified by occasional parity changes in reaction to fundamental disequilibria), under which the Western world operated from 1945 until 1971. (The next chapter explains why the Bretton Woods system finally broke down in 1971.)

The fixed exchange rate element within the present global system is principally represented by the European Exchange Rate Mechanism (ERM), which aims to limit the fluctuation of exchange rates of the member countries of the European Community. The exchange rate limits allow most members maximum movements of ±2.25% of the fixed values for each pair of currencies (±6% for the UK in the initial stage of its ERM membership). To maintain currencies in this relationship requires occasional direct intervention in the foreign currency markets, but even more crucially it involves a pattern of domestic interest rates which will ensure that currencies stay within their bands; and, more significantly, it also involves a degree of convergence in terms of macroeconomic performance.

Convergence in economic performance is clearly essential before the final stage of economic and monetary union (EMU), namely the creation of a single currency for participating countries, can take place. The Maastricht agreement of December 1991 brought this into sharper focus by establishing a timetable for full EMU, and setting convergence criteria. If the majority of member states fulfil the convergence criteria shown below, monetary union will begin in 1997. If, as is likely, the majority of members do not pass the convergence tests, a minority who do pass the tests will be free to form a monetary union in 1999. The convergence criteria are:

- a consumer price inflation rate within 1.5 percentage points of the three lowest national rates in the previous year
- a long-term interest rate within 2 percentage points of the three lowest members in the previous year
- a budget deficit of 3% or less of GDP *or* a gross public debt which does not exceed 60% of GDP – unless it is falling 'at a satisfactory pace'

– an exchange rate which has been a member of the narrow **ERM** band for at least two years without realignment.

The bi-lateral relationships between the US dollar, the yen and the ERM currencies allow for reasonably free floating – there are no formal bands within which these currencies are required to move. However, as mentioned earlier, governments are reluctant to allow exchange rates to be determined entirely by market forces. Thus, since the late 1970s, in a succession of meetings of ministers of the G7 (the seven largest Western industrialized economies: the US, Japan, Germany, France, the UK, Italy and Canada), there has been frequent agreement regarding the broad exchange rate levels, or bands, which are considered most beneficial to the international economy. Such agreement has only occasionally been supplemented by specific policy action in terms of market intervention or other measures, for example, through the co-ordinated moving of interest rates. On the whole, international efforts to manage exchange rates at a global level have had only limited success since national interests have often diverged.

Long-term trends in exchange rates

Whatever formal regime is in force, the broad pattern of exchange rates in the long-term is determined by market forces, though official policy is a very important factor in the marketplace. Direct intervention can exert a powerful impact only if backed by other policy measures likely to affect the demand/supply balance in the market. As for interest rate differentials, they are undoubtedly the most powerful factor affecting exchange rates over the short term; but over the medium and long term, other factors come into play, most importantly the balance of payments on both current and capital account, and inflation differentials. In general, if the authorities attempt to hold exchange rates above or below their market equilibrium levels in defiance of basic fundamentals, imbalances are likely to emerge (e.g. external deficits, unemployment or inflation), which will force the authorities either to devalue or revalue their currencies or to change policy in another respect.

The theory of purchasing power parity (PPP) highlights the importance of differences in relative inflation rates in determining long-term movements in exchange rates. According to the theory, the equilibrium exchange rate between any two currencies is that rate which equalizes the domestic purchasing power of those currencies. For example, if a basket of tradeable goods is priced at £100 in the UK and DM300 in Germany, then the PPP rate of exchange is £1 = DM3. If over a long period, inflation in the UK means that the same basket costs £200, while prices have remained stable in Germany, then the PPP rate of exchange is £2 = DM3. In these circumstances, sterling's exchange rate has adjusted by exactly the amount required to compensate for domestic inflation and to maintain the competitiveness of British goods in international markets. Figure 8.1 shows that PPP has actually worked remarkably well in practice. Over the period 1960–88, those countries with the highest rates of inflation have seen the sharpest declines in the exchange value of their currencies.

In interpreting PPP, it is important to bear in mind that in the real world the theory is subject to many qualifications and that it can only work over very long periods, say 6–7 years or more. Also, there exist various impediments to international trade, such as transport costs, which detract from the ability of PPP to explain exchange rate movements fully. The strict theory is only valid for goods and services which are traded internationally, so that the general level of prices (expressed, say, in comparing retail price within countries) may not accurately reflect trends in the traded goods sector. Finally, PPP does not take account of capital movements. These have become increasingly important in determining exchange rate movements, since they are the key force in the demand/supply balance for assets in a global economy where capital flows are considerably larger than trade flows.

The current account is nevertheless still regarded as a particularly

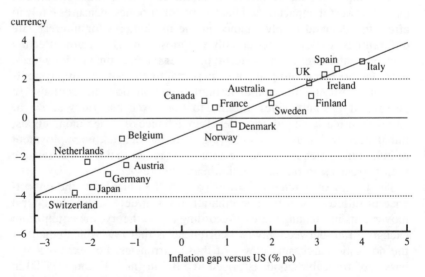

Figure 8.1 PPP in practice, 1960–88

important factor in determining exchange rate movements, with a persistent surplus putting upward pressure on the rate, while a persistent deficit is evidence of economic weakness and is normally expected to have the opposite effect. However, the globalization of the capital markets has made it easier for large external deficits to be financed over many years without forcing exchange rate adjustments.

Despite its shortcomings, the PPP theory produces a very convincing description and plausible explanation of exchange rate movements over the past two decades, and provides a useful guide to what the long-run equilibrium position should be between two currencies whose domestic inflation rates differ persistently.

The relationship between interest and exchange rates

Although it is virtually impossible to prove that there is a causal relationship between inflation and exchange rates, the assertion that long-term exchange rate movements are determined by inflation differentials is a tenable starting point. Short- and medium-term movements, on the other hand, reflect many factors including official intervention, interest rate differentials and deficits/surpluses in a country's international balance of trade and capital flows. However, in order to interpret the role of interest rates correctly, it is important to judge whether they are set by policy action, aimed at changing basic economic conditions, or whether they simply reflect the market's judgement of underlying and persistent differences in economic performance. For example, a 3% gap between UK and German interest rates may be a key part of British anti-inflation policy which, if successful, will result in UK interest rates coming down to German levels and in sterling remaining stable against the DM once inflation differentials have been eliminated. Alternatively, the same interest rate gap could, in other circumstances, reflect market perceptions that the inflation gap between the two countries will persist, and that the interest rate differential is necessary to compensate for the future devaluation of sterling. In other words, the overall policy content is all-important.

Disappointment in inflation performances during the 1970s and the 1980s has revived the attractions of currency stability through systems such as the ERM. However, there is a cost to countries participating in a fixed or managed rate system, since governments unilaterally forego changes in the exchange rate as a tool of policy. This can have unfavourable short- and medium-term consequences for trade competitiveness and for the level of employment. The advantage to the economy is that the fixed rate system enhances the prospects of long-term price stability by preventing governments from devaluing to obtain a short-term gain in terms of a boost to exports and output.

Countries which have joined the ERM have accepted this trade-off, using interest rate differentials to counteract initially the impact of different rates of inflation on their currencies. They have ultimately validated this policy by longer-term convergence in inflation rates and, in so doing also permitting the interest gap to narrow and in some cases eventually disappear. Table 8.1 illustrates the effect of interest rates in helping gradually to eliminate the fundamental inflation imbalances between two countries in the system, Germany and France. Table 8.2 shows that the policy has been less successful in the case of Italy, where the inflation gap has narrowed, but not disappeared.

The lira joined the ERM at the system's inception in March 1979. Given Italy's inflation record, the lira was allowed a 6% margin either side of its central parity, compared with 2.25% for other members. In order to support the currency in this band, high interest rates were offered on Italian assets to compensate for inflation and the possibility of capital loss. Nevertheless, in the early years of the ERM, a number of realignments were necessary as pressure built up as a result of divergent economic performance, notably Italy's persistently high inflation rate and huge public debt. Changes in the lira/DM rate are shown in column 4 of Table 8.2. However, the frequency and magnitude of the lira's devaluations has diminished as the inflation performance of the two countries has converged. In January 1990, the Italian currency moved into the narrower ±2.25% fluctuation band of the ERM.

As explained earlier, there is also a mechanistic relationship between interest rates and exchange rates operating through the forward discount or premiums in the forex market. As Table 8.3 illustrates, the differential between interest rates in different countries is reflected precisely in the premiums and discounts offered on forward exchange rates. The interest rates used in Table 8.3 are eurocurrency rates, which are virtually identical to rates in the domestic markets of the currencies selected. The cost of forward cover for all currencies considered is expressed as a discount against the US dollar. The same was true on the date selected for all major currencies, since at the time dollar interest rates were the lowest in the OECD area. The following points should elucidate the main conclusion to be drawn from Table 8.3 which is that after subtracting the cost of forward cover for each currency from the relevant interest rate, one is left with the interest rate on US dollars. In other words, the forward premium or discount equalizes the interest rate differential.

Table 8.1   Relationship between interest rates policy and exchange rates – Deutschmark and French franc

	Inflation (% pa) Germany	France	Interest rate differential (%)*	Exchange rate FrFr/DM (end-year)
1979	4.1	10.7	n.a.	2.32
1980	5.4	13.2	2.19	2.31
1981	6.3	13.4	6.13	2.53
1982	5.3	11.8	19.06	2.83
1983	3.3	9.6	7.44	3.05
1984	2.4	7.5	5.19	3.06
1985	2.2	5.7	8.44	3.06
1986	−0.1	2.5	5.69	3.28
1987	0.2	3.3	5.50	3.39
1988	1.3	2.7	3.25	3.42
1989	2.8	3.5	3.06	3.42
1990	2.7	3.4	0.89	3.40
1991	3.5	3.1	nil	3.41

*End-year difference between 3-month eurocurrency rates for the Deutschmark and French franc. Figures shown are French franc rates less Deutschmark rates

Table 8.2   Relationship between interest rates policy and exchange rates – Deutschmark and lira

	Inflation (% pa) Germany	Italy	Interest rate differential (%)*	Exchange rate lire/DM (end-year)
1979	4.1	14.8	n.a.	465
1980	5.4	21.0	9.63	474
1981	6.3	17.9	13.25	534
1982	5.3	16.5	19.25	576
1983	3.3	14.7	10.94	606
1984	2.4	10.8	8.94	616
1985	2.2	9.2	12.44	681
1986	−0.1	5.9	6.56	693
1987	0.2	4.7	8.25	736
1988	1.3	5.0	6.50	737
1989	2.8	6.3	4.56	743
1990	2.7	6.1	2.81	754
1991	3.5	6.4	1.80	747

*End-year difference between 3-month eurocurrency rates for the Deutschmark and lira. Figures shown are lire rates less Deutschmark rates

Table 8.3   Interest rates and forward cover

Currency	Eurocurrency rates (3-months %)	Cost of forward cover against US$ %
US dollar	5.38	–
Sterling	10.28	4.83 discount
Deutschmark	9.38	4.03 discount
Yen	6.53	1.10 discount

Rates as at October 1991 expressed as % per annum

1. Since UK rates are higher than dollar rates, it would be profitable for investors to exchange dollars for sterling, so long as the exchange rate between the two currencies did not move against the pound more than the interest rate differential. If the pound's exchange value against the dollar fell between the time the investment was made and the repayment date, the interest advantage could be completely eroded.
2. In order to protect against such an exchange rate risk, investors take the precaution of forward cover. This means that in this case, they sell sterling for dollars ahead of the ultimate maturity of the sterling investment, to fix the rate at the current level.
3. Forward cover has a cost (in the case of sterling in this example an annual rate of 4.83%) and when this is deducted from sterling rates, the difference between sterling and dollar rates is negligible. Investors who do not cover deals in this way are taking a gamble on what is going to happen to spot exchange rates.
4. Arbitrage ensures that the cost of forward cover erodes the interest rate differential. This may seem to imply that there is no advantage in switching into other currencies, but conditions are always changing and opportunities arising.

While very important in currency trading, the forward exchange market does not tell us anything about causal relationships, neither does it necessarily provide a good prediction of the future spot rate for currencies. A currency can trade at a forward discount, but can on occasion appreciate over the period to which the discount relates.

International aspects of long-term interest rate determination

The close and important connection between exchange rates and interest rates focuses on short-term interest rate movements. Reference was made on page 60 to the international influence on long-term rates, an area less crucial than the exchange rate/interest rate relationship, but one which is nevertheless worth considering.

The global demand/supply balance for capital inevitably impacts on long-term interest rates in domestic economies, given the close integration of major financial markets. Thus, the factors determining the global balance will ultimately affect domestic rates. Factors to be considered are: the savings ratio in developed countries; total investment spending in those countries; the totality of OECD budget deficits; and the demands for capital of other major country groups – the Eastern bloc and the developing countries. These magnitudes are difficult to quantify, but are important determinants of long-term rates. If these factors in combination seem likely to produce a shortage of capital, as some have suggested, then long-term interest rates in domestic markets are likely to rise.

Conclusion

In a world where economic performance between trading partners varies appreciably, and where countries operate in a fixed rate regime such as the EMS or more generally under managed floating exchange rates, there is an important link between the level and trend of interest rates and exchange rates. This chapter has illustrated how interest rate differentials can counteract for long periods the impact on exchange rates of different inflation performances, and can in some cases ultimately help produce convergence of both inflation and interest rates. The EMS countries have provided an example of successful co-operation in directing interest rate policy towards the goal of attaining exchange rate stability. The huge volume of international trade and capital flows in the increasingly integrated global economy highlights the importance of the relationship between interest rates and exchange rates.

CHAPTER 9

Historical trends in interest rates

A good understanding of past trends is a key ingredient in any systematic attempt to predict future movements in interest rates. This chapter provides an examination of the course of interest rates in major economies over the past three decades. Patterns have changed markedly over the period due to the following main factors: (1) fluctuations in inflation; (2) structural changes in the international background and developments in economic thinking; (3) the thorough reassessment of policy aims and instruments on the part of most major governments; (4) the liberalization and internationalization of major capital markets, and (5) trends in global investment and savings patterns. Government policy and the investment/saving balance are the major determinants of real interest rates, and we shall see in the course of this review how real rates have moved from being at very low (or even negative) levels during the 1960s and much of the 1970s, to high levels in the 1980s and 1990s.

The main trends since the early 1960s

1960–65

During the early 1960s, the world was still operating reasonably successfully within the framework of the Bretton Woods system of quasi-fixed exchange rates, under which currencies were permitted to fluctuate only within narrow bands of 1% around agreed par values. Realignments were permitted only in order to correct 'fundamental disequilibria' and required the agreement of the International Monetary Fund (IMF), the institution established to oversee the operation of the Bretton Woods arrangements. Part of the IMF's role was to provide financial assistance to member countries experiencing balance of payments difficulties, with the aim of helping them correct such problems without having to resort to trade or payments restrictions and without requiring sizeable exchange rate realignments. Financial assistance from the IMF, coupled with the fact that inflation differentials were generally small, meant that currency realignments during the early 1960s were relatively infrequent. This period marked the high point of the relative exchange rate stability that existed under the Bretton Woods system. In that environment, interest rates were reasonably low and stable both in nominal and real terms, as illustrated in Figures 9.1–9.3.

In the charts used in this chapter to illustrate interest rate trends, the rates used are end-year short-term (3-month) money market rates. The overall trend in long-term rates has been similar throughout the period. Long-term rates have generally been around 1% higher than short-term rates as would be expected if the shape of the yield curve is normal, i.e. upward sloping. The real rate of interest shown below each of these charts has been calculated by deducting from nominal rates the current annual rate of inflation, measured by 12-month changes in consumer or retail prices for each period. Conceptually, real rates should be calculated using expected inflation but, as mentioned in Chapter 3, this is difficult to gauge.
Note that the shaded area in figures 9.1–9.15 indicates the real rate of interest.

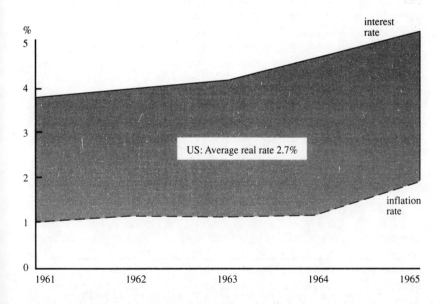

Figure 9.1 Real interest rates 1961–65 in the US

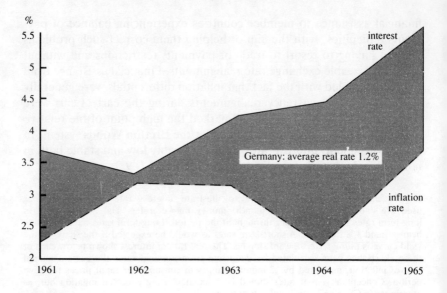

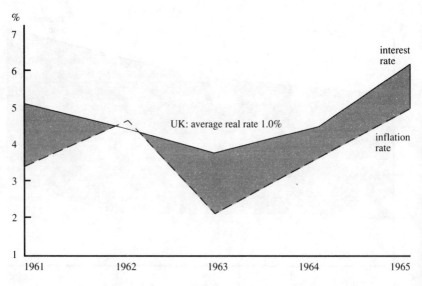

Figure 9.2 Real interest rates 1961–65 in Germany and the UK

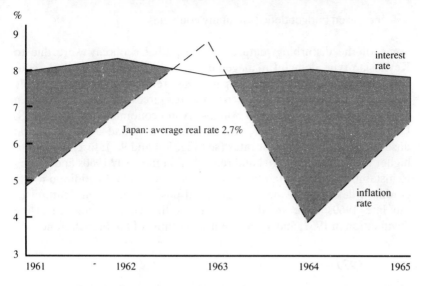

Figure 9.3 Real interest rates 1961–65 in Japan

1966–70

The Bretton Woods structure came under increasing pressure in the second half of the 1960s. The dominant currency in the system since the end of the Second World War had been the US dollar, reflecting the overwhelming strength of the US economy. The par value of most currencies in the system was pegged to the dollar, while the dollar itself was pegged to gold. However, a number of factors combined to weaken the dollar's strength and its pivotal role in the system as the decade drew to a close:

- the economic strengthening of Germany and Japan and their emergence as major trading nations, with increasingly powerful currencies. These, however, were pegged to the dollar at an exchange rate which necessitated a reassessment
- the widening external deficit of the US, and the refusal of the authorities to devalue the dollar or to introduce restrictive economic policies to curb the deficit – a policy often described as 'benign neglect' in relation to the external position
- a general rise in inflation in the OECD area and the emergence of fairly sizeable gaps between inflation rates in various countries

73

– increased budget deficits in many countries.

Some of the disturbing features in the global economy were due to Keynesian-type demand management policies, mainly aimed at reducing unemployment. Their impact was reinforced by the sharply increased pressure on world economic resources due to the Vietnam War, particularly in the main Anglo-Saxon economies such as the US, UK and Canada. However, these features also had a more general unsettling effect on interest rates (see Fig. 9.4 and 9.5), forcing them to higher levels, both nominal and real, than in the early 1960s and adding to instability and uncertainty in the financial markets. In addition to the gradual weakening of the US's financial position, the main features of the late 1960s were steady pressure on the UK, forcing a sterling devaluation in 1967, and a persistent weakening of the French franc.

1971–75

Market pressures on the dollar built up during 1969–71, as overseas holders sold dollars for gold and other currencies. In August 1971, the position was finally considered to be untenable by the US authorities and President Nixon suspended the agreement for convertibility of the dollar into gold at the fixed rate of $35 an ounce which had underpinned the Bretton Woods system. Following this move, currencies floated on a managed basis but without any formal structure. In December 1971, the Smithsonian Conference reached agreement on a new fixed exchange rate regime. Most major currencies were revalued against the dollar, the fluctuation band around dollar parities was widened to 2.25%, and the official dollar price of gold was raised. However, this arrangement proved short-lived. Balance of payments pressures forced the UK in July 1972 to abandon its attempt to join the European Currency bloc known as the 'snake', and this precipitated a sterling devaluation and a subsequent managed float. This proved to be a prelude to pressures on other currencies. There were further revaluations of the yen and the Deutschmark in February, but the markets were not convinced that the new exchange rates were sustainable. By March 1973, all major currencies were operating under a managed floating arrangement.

Two other important influences on the course of interest rates during the 1970s emerged during the early years of the decade. The OPEC oil price rise of late 1973/early 1974, which occurred at a time of synchronized expansion in the global economy, had an immediate and dramatic effect leading to a sharp acceleration of inflation, as illustrated in Figure 9.6 and 9.7. However, rather unusually and ominously, this upsurge in inflation also coincided with recession or low growth, a

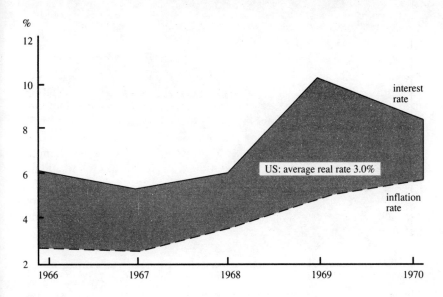

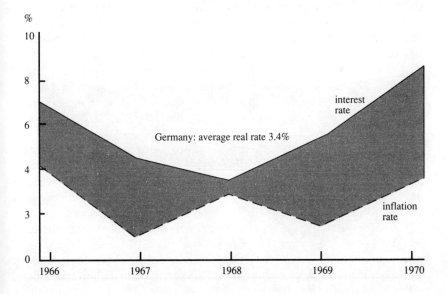

Figure 9.4 Real interest rates 1966–70 in the US and Germany

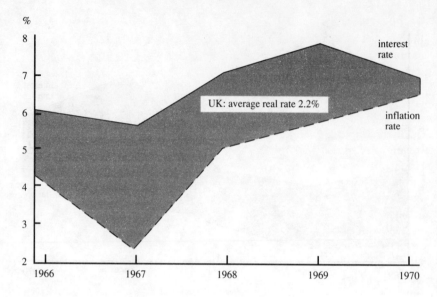

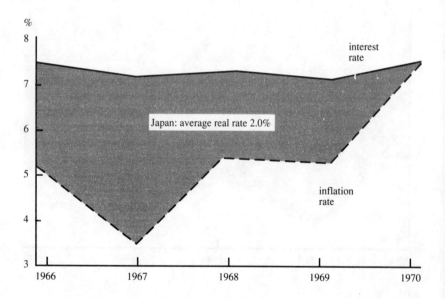

Figure 9.5 Real interest rates 1966–70 in the UK and Japan

phenomenon that came to be known as 'stagflation'. The divergent impact on inflation in various countries, coupled with rapid changes in countries' balance of payments positions, emphasized the difficulty of returning to a fixed exchange rate system.

The high rates of inflation, triggered by the oil price increase of late 1973 and early 1974, caused nominal interest rates to rise sharply and to remain high throughout 1974 and much of 1975. They reached historically high levels in some countries, including the UK, but this did not result in a rise in real rates, as can be seen from Figure 9.6 and 9.7. Indeed, in many instances real rates became negative. This was because monetary and fiscal policies at this time remained expansionary, as governments were more concerned with countering the recessionary effects of the oil shock than the inflation effects.

An additional factor which emerged during this period, and one which had important repercussions for interest rates during the late 1970s, was the rise of monetarism as a key influence on domestic economic management. This followed growing disillusionment in the late 1960s with Keynesian demand management policies, its apparent ineffectiveness in countering inflation, and its inability to produce steady non-inflationary economic growth. There was a crucial change at about this time in economists' thinking about monetary policy, a policy tool which since the end of the Second World War had played a subordinate role to fiscal policy in economic management. As explained in Chapter 1, monetarism was based on a revival of the theory that inflation is fundamentally a monetary phenomenon and that, therefore, monetary factors are crucial in determining macroeconomic movements and, in particular, are closely associated with inflation. The implication of this approach involved much greater emphasis on controlling the rate of growth of money supply, with the authorities establishing in the early 1970s a framework for operations which would enable them to influence effectively the rate of growth of monetary aggregates.

As the decade progressed, monetarist ideas and policies exerted progressively greater influence on the level of interest rates on both sides of the Atlantic. The authorities in Germany were among the first to announce firm monetary targets, while the US government began publishing target ranges for various definitions of the money supply in January 1974. Targets have been announced for every year since then. Targets were first published in the UK in 1976, and in France in 1977. For consideration of the techniques used and an assessment of monetary policy in the US and the UK, see Chapters 6 and 7. The effect on interest rates is examined in the section below which covers the second half of the 1970s.

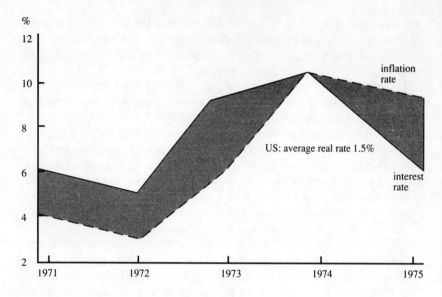

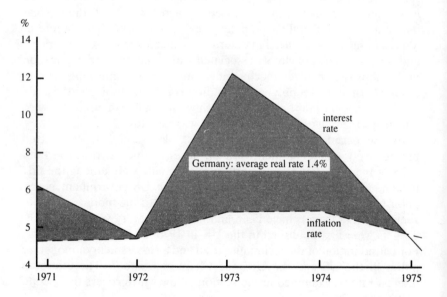

Figure 9.6 Real interest rates 1971–75 in the US and Germany

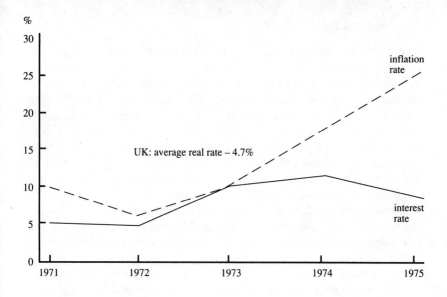

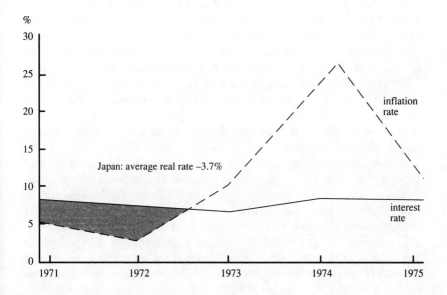

Figure 9.7 Real interest rates 1971–75 in the UK and Japan

1976–80

The inflationary impact of the first OPEC oil price shock had been only partially overcome by the mid-seventies, with inflation in 1976 still running at almost 6% in the US, over 9% in Japan and France, and around 16% in the UK. Economic policy remained expansionary in 1975/76, on the grounds that it was still necessary to offset the deflationary effects of the OPEC-induced recession. These policies meant that the UK, at least, was now in a serious economic situation. Not only was inflation rampant, but the balance of payments position was deteriorating rapidly. This forced the UK government to enter into negotiations with the IMF for financial assistance. The result was a tightening of monetary policy, and included the introduction of targets for monetary expansion to comply with IMF conditions. Policy was also becoming more restrictive in the US, in response to rising inflation and dollar weakness. This policy tightening is highlighted in Figure 9.4, which shows a sharp rise in interest rates towards the end of the decade and the emergence, for the first time since the Second World War, of real interest rates in some major economies well above the long-run historical average of around 2.5%.

Real interest rates have generally remained high in major countries since the mid-1970s, with the events of 1979 being of especial significance. Real interest rates in the US rose particularly sharply in that year, following the appointment of Mr Paul Volcker as Chairman of the Federal Reserve System. The failure of the US government to deal with the growing fiscal deficit, rising inflation and a widening current account shortfall led to the implementation by the independent Fed (see Chap. 7) under Mr Volcker of a very tight monetary policy. The year 1979 also saw the election in the UK of a Conservative government under Mrs Thatcher committed to a monetarist economic strategy which involved strict control of the monetary aggregates (as well as of public expenditure and of the budget deficit) in order to bring inflation effectively under control.

A third major event of 1979 was the second OPEC oil price rise following the Islamic revolution in Iran and the removal of the Shah. With policy in both the US and the UK now firmly directed at controlling inflation, and with Japan determined not to allow a repeat of the inflationary upsurge of the 1973 oil shock, it was not surprising that the response of governments was quite different from that which characterized the 1973–75 period. Instead of attempting to protect world economic growth by boosting demand, governments on this occasion put the fight against inflation as their main economic objective. Monetary policy was tightened and real interest rates rose sharply,

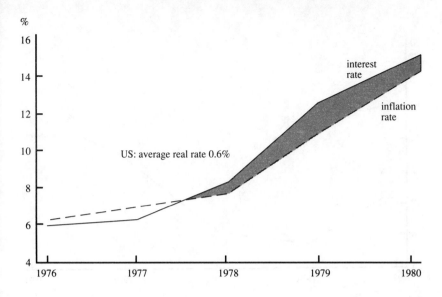

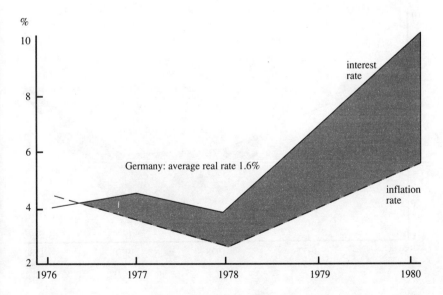

Figure 9.8 Real interest rates 1976–80 in the US and Germany

HISTORICAL TRENDS IN INTEREST RATES

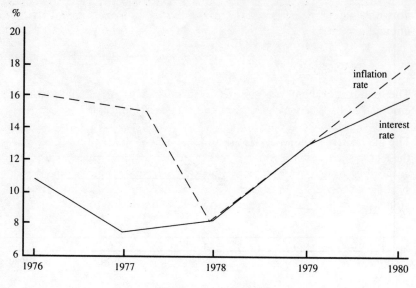

UK: average real rate –2.8%

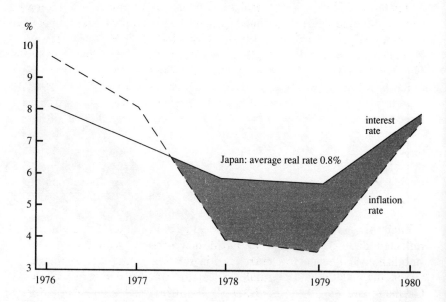

Figure 9.9 Real interest rates 1976–80 in the UK and Japan

notwithstanding the adverse effect on output and the consequent rise in unemployment.

1981–85

The pattern of high real interest rates in major economies which emerged in 1979 was consolidated and reinforced in the first half of the 1980s. This reflected tight monetary policies in the OECD countries. The global recession reached its low point in 1982 (1981 in the UK) and the early stages of the upturn were cautious and subdued, with the authorities relying on monetary policy to squeeze inflation out of the system. At the same time, it was evident that significant changes in the global supply of savings and demand for capital were occurring.

Monetary policy

In the US, the election of Mr Reagan as President in 1980 reinforced the shift towards monetarist policies. However, because of Mr Reagan's commitment to lower taxation, it also produced the mix of a highly expansionary fiscal but a restrictive monetary stance which remained a prominent feature of policy, and ensured that interest rates remained at a high level. The massive Federal budget deficit of around $200 billion a year at that time was accompanied by tight money supply target ranges – 6–9% for M2, for example, in 1984 – which allowed the Fed little leeway in reducing interest rates even though inflation was moderating sharply. One consequence of this policy imbalance was a sharp rise in the US dollar, resulting in a very large increase in the US external deficit.

In the UK, the Conservative Government persisted with its strategy aimed at reducing inflation through strict monetary control, setting out its approach in the Medium-Term Financial Strategy (MTFS) introduced in 1980. The MTFS contained targets to reduce the rate of monetary growth, public spending, taxation and the fiscal deficit year-by-year. The wholehearted commitment to monetarism underpinning this strategy necessarily involved reliance on high interest rates, and also involved a prolonged period of high unemployment.

High interest rates in France, Italy and several other EC countries reflected their commitment to ERM membership, with the aim of stabilizing their respective currencies in relation to the Deutschmark. Given the inflation differential with major trading partners such as Germany and the Netherlands, these countries were obliged to offer high interest rates to support their currencies.

Savings and investment

Figure 9.10 illustrates a trend which emerged in the 1970s and continued for most of the 1980s, namely a steady decline in savings as a percentage of GDP in the OECD area. Gross savings reached a peak in 1973 at 26% of GDP, and then declined fairly steadily until the mid-1980s. For net saving (after deducting depreciation) the decline is even more marked, from a peak of 17% of GNP in 1973 to 8% in 1983, reflecting a sizeable increase in depreciation charges over the period.

The decline in the volume of savings in relation to GDP was accompanied during the first half of the 1980s by significant increases in the demand for capital, largely from within the OECD. This increase was stimulated by a strong rise in the profitability of investment. This was partly due to the tax cuts implemented during President Reagan's first term in office, a measure which contributed to the huge US budget deficit. After a negative performance in the 1970s, the average real capital gain in the period 1982 to 1986 is estimated at 15% a year. On the assumption that such a rise would automatically generate a substantial increase in the demand for investment funds, the real rate of interest also rose, and this factor helps to explain the high positive level of real rates seen during the first half of the 1980s (Figs 9.11–9.13).

1986–91

The demand for capital remained strong in the second half of the 1980s, exerting continued upward pressure on real interest rates. However, the anti-inflation policies of the early 1980s underwent a temporary change in the years 1986–88 which offset the impact of demand/supply factors during this period, and resulted in lower levels of real interest rates.

The first reason for the policy shift was cyclical. Inflationary pressures eased considerably in 1986 and 1987, with consumer prices in 1986 rising by only 2% in the US and 6% in Japan, and actually falling by 0.1% in Germany. Some governments (particularly in the Anglo-Saxon economies) relaxed, somewhat prematurely, their concern with strict anti-inflation policies.

The second factor reflected the large-scale deregulation and financial innovation of the early 1980s which produced a huge expansion of personal and company lending. This in turn caused major difficulties in interpreting changes in monetary aggregates, including the fact that the relationship between money supply growth and inflation no longer appeared to hold. As a result, the previous importance of changes in broad money aggregates in policy formulation was downgraded in several major OECD countries from the mid-1980s, and this

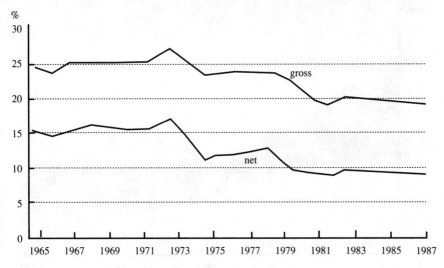

Source: Organization for Economic Cooperation and Development *National Accounts.*
Gross saving as percentage of GNP; net saving as percentage of national income

Figure 9.10 National saving rates, 1965–87 (in percentages)

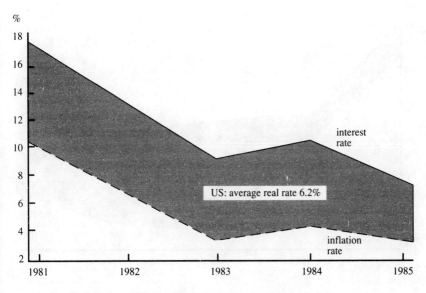

Figure 9.11 Real interest rates 1981–85 in the US

85

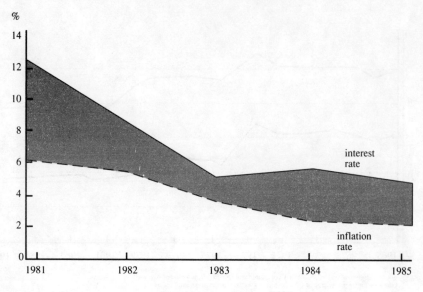

Germany: average real rate 3.7%

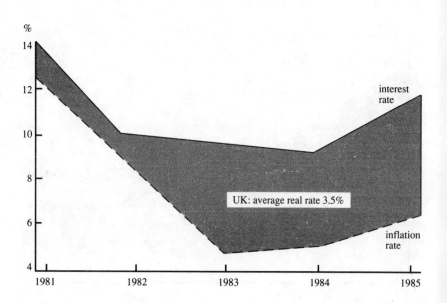

Figure 9.12 Real interest rates 1981–85 in Germany and the UK

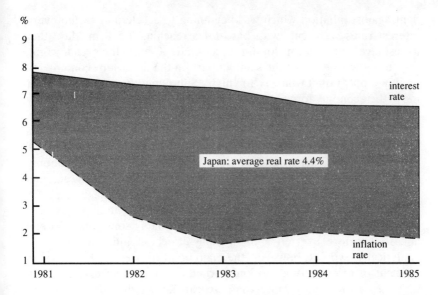

Figure 9.13 Real interest rates 1981–85 in Japan

contributed to a departure from the application of strict monetarist principles. With hindsight, this can be seen to have resulted in major policy mistakes and a subsequent upsurge in inflation.

A third factor which temporarily reinforced the policy shift was the international response to the stockmarket crash of October 1987, which involved the injection of liquidity into the system on the part of many OECD area central banks in order to avert any threat to economic growth. This was an understandable policy error, but one which contributed to the subsequent inflationary upsurge.

In the UK, the erratic behaviour of the broad money supply measures meant that the targets set under the MTFS required constant upward adjustment. In 1987, the Treasury abandoned the targeting of broad money altogether. Afterwards, policy was formulated in the light of a broader range of indicators, including the exchange rate. One important consequence was an intellectual shift from domestic to international monetarism. Sterling's performance against the Deutschmark became a dominant constraint on interest rate policy, and one which had the potential to conflict on occasion with domestic considerations. This dilemma arose in 1988.

For much of 1987 and the early weeks of 1988, sterling appeared to shadow the Deutschmark. In March 1988, sterling began to strengthen and the government was faced with conflicting objectives of exchange rate stability (which at the time required a reduction in rates) and the fight against inflation which was beginning to accelerate. In the event, interest rates were cut, with base rates reaching 7.5% in May, their lowest level in real terms for almost a decade. Clearly the exchange rate was 'too low' and it had the same impact on the domestic economy as a money supply target which is 'too high'. Subsequently, serious overheating in the economy forced the government to raise interest rates sharply. With bank base rates at 15% by the end of 1989, the decade ended with the very high real levels seen in the early 1980s. Thereafter, nominal rates declined following sterling's entry into the ERM in October 1990 and against the background of deep recession in the UK economy. However, with inflation also falling sharply, real interest rates remained relatively high throughout 1991.

The main difference between the 1988 and 1991 Deutschmark targets for sterling is that in 1991 the target was probably somewhat too high and it therefore exerted a dampening effect on inflation. From an analytical viewpoint, however, the main point to stress is that there are no clear or prior methods to know whether a particular exchange rate target is 'correct' any more than we can know whether a particular money supply target is right. Judgement must still play a key role.

In the US, monetary policy became more accommodating between 1985 and 1987 in response to a modest weakening in economic activity and against a background of low inflation. As demand and price pressures re-emerged in the later years of the decade, real interest rates again became strongly positive, before declining again from mid-1990 in response to slackening economic growth and a sharp deceleration in credit expansion. For much of the second half of 1991, as the Fed attempted to pull the economy out of recession, short-term interest rates stood at little over 5%, implying real rates of around 1%.

In the EC, a feature of interest rate performance in the early 1990s has been the culmination of a decade of increasing convergence, particularly of short-term rates. As Table 9.1 shows, there was very little

Table 9.1   3-month eurocurrency rates in EC countries

% End-October 1991	
Belgium	9.25
Denmark	9.44
France	9.13
Germany	9.44
Holland	9.31
Italy	11.00
Spain	12.60
UK	10.50

difference among rates in the 'core' EC economies at the end of 1991 and the differential between rates in these countries and the remainder of the EC was very low compared to the level seen earlier in the decade. However, the erosion of interest rate differentials may not be sustainable, nor does it imply that sufficient convergence of economic performance has yet been achieved to make monetary union possible within the next few years.

A final point to consider in this review of monetary developments in the late 1980s and early 1990s is the sharp deceleration in OECD money supply growth during 1991. This phenomenon largely reflects demand problems – the fact that borrowers continue to feel excessively indebted – rather than supply problems through unwillingness to lend on the part of the banking system. The sharp decline in demand for credit has given rise in some quarters to fears of global recession or serious depression. Such fears are probably exaggerated. On this occasion, monetary slowdown is a coincidental indicator reflecting the financial retrenchment of the corporate and personal sectors, and is not a lead indicator foreshadowing further declines in activity. Nevertheless, there is a policy difficulty for central banks in some of the main countries concerned: the US, the UK and Japan. Given the UK's commitment to ERM membership, there is limited scope for a large reduction in interest rates. The US and Japan do, however, have the option of reducing rates significantly to encourage borrowers and thus assist a revival in economic activity. This issue will have considerable implications for the level of real interest rates in some major economies in the next few years. (See Figure. 9.14 pp. 90–1).

Conclusion

The historical overview provided in this chapter has highlighted the main determinants of interest rate trends during the past 30 years. Understanding the past provides a useful basis for forecasting the future, and the examination of interest rate trends and their causes over a long period will prove of great assistance when, in Chapter 12, we turn our attention to forecasting trends over the next few years.

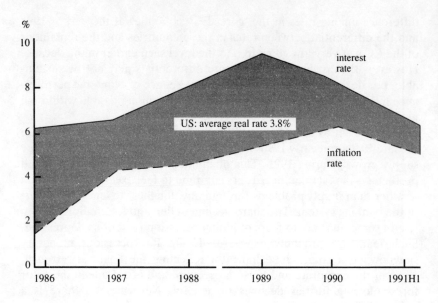

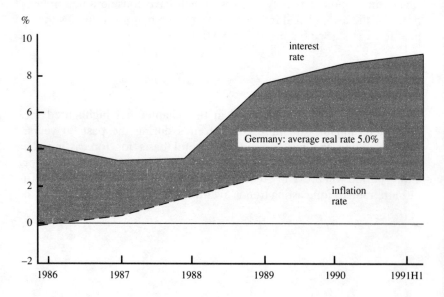

Figure 9.14 Real interest rates 1986–91 in the US and Germany

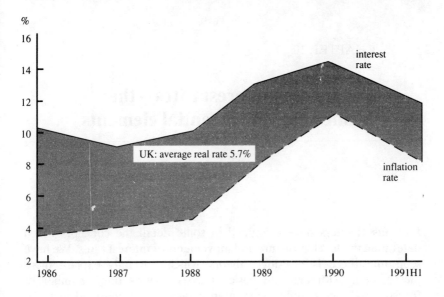

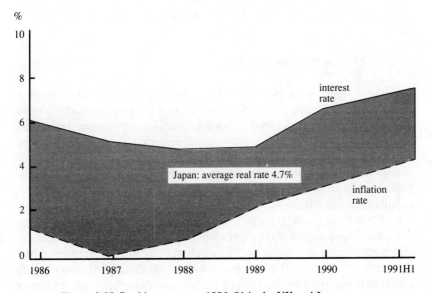

Figure 9.15 Real interest rates 1986–91 in the UK and Japan

CHAPTER 10

Forecasting interest rates – the framework and essential elements

Previous chapters have examined in some detail the concepts which determine the level, structure and movements of interest rates. We have seen that there is no single theory which can fully explain these phenomena. Although the basic analysis focuses on a number of fundamental factors influencing interest rates, the precise linkages and channels of causation vary considerably in practice, depending among other things on changes in expectations, which can neither be predicted nor, indeed, even observed accurately. In addition, interest rates are affected by specific government actions, which exert a powerful influence at the short end of the maturity spectrum. This chapter brings together the various elements necessary to understand movements in interest rates, and shows their relevance in projecting future trends.

The factors to consider

Forecasting interest rates, whether it is done implicitly or in an explicit manner, is an essential part of the decision-making process in which most business people are involved. Bankers, investors, corporate treasurers and money market dealers are constantly required to take a view about future interest rate movements over different maturities and periods of time. For money market participants, the time horizon is short, and is measured in days or weeks. Investors, whether business or personal, usually take a much longer view. The period to which the forecast relates is highly relevant in determining the factors that the forecaster needs to consider. The focus of this chapter will be to highlight the differences in emphasis placed on various factors when making interest rate forecasts. A matrix approach will be adopted, which will distinguish, on the one hand, between the time horizon of the forecast (whether shorter term or longer term) and, on the other hand, the maturity under consideration (i.e. whether the rate applies to short-term funds or funds with a long period to maturity). Table 10.1 indicates the relevant factors and the rest of this chapter follows this framework.

Table 10.1   Matrix for interest rate forecasts: the factors to consider

	Short-term rates	Long-term rates
Short-term forecast	Monetary policy Demand/supply factors Market expectations of official action	Demand/supply factors Market expectations of inflation trends
Long-term forecast	Inflation Monetary policy Demand/supply factors Economic cycle	Inflation Demand/supply factors Economic cycle

Factors to consider in the short-term forecast

Those who provide or use interest rate forecasts are primarily concerned with the actual level of nominal rates. However, as shown in Chapter 3, this can be conceptually separated into two elements: inflation and the real rate of interest. In the short-term forecast of nominal rates (say, for the period up to three months ahead), the rate of inflation may normally be considered as 'given', since inflation changes only slowly over a period of a few weeks. The fact that a major component of nominal interest rates can be taken for granted should in theory make the job of short-term forecasting easier and more accurate when compared with predictions for longer periods, which necessarily also involve a forecast of inflation. However, these advantages are sometimes outweighed by the occasional sharp volatility of short-term movements which can be disregarded in a long-term forecast.

In looking at the short-term course of interest rates, the forecaster will focus on three sets of factors. Firstly, there is a need to consider developments which impinge directly on the overall stance of monetary policy, and the specific factors used by the authorities to influence interest rates. These factors will act primarily on the short end of the spectrum (i.e. maturities up to 3–6 months), but with a ripple effect across the spectrum which could also affect longer-term rates. Secondly, short-term influences on the demand for and supply of funds need to be considered.

These factors are likely to affect both short- and long-term interest rates. Thirdly, market expectations must be taken into account. Such expectations influence the level of rates as well as the shape of the yield curve, and could themselves be determined by factors ranging from global geo-political events to perceptions about the government's intentions.

Monetary policy factors

Changes in interest rates are a major weapon used by the authorities when seeking to achieve monetary policy targets. These targets (often referred to as intermediate targets on the road towards the ultimate goal of reduced inflation) include controlling the growth of the money supply, limiting the demand for credit and influencing the exchange rate. Any development likely to elicit a response from the authorities in the form of an interest rate change to help achieve the above goals clearly has to be taken into account in the short-term forecast. The following are some of the important developments that could prompt the authorities to act on short-term interest rates:

– monetary growth exceeding or undershooting set targets
– excessive expansion or, more unusually, undue slack in personal or corporate borrowing
– economic imbalances manifested in a sudden worsening in the country's inflation or its balance of payments position
– imbalances reflected in recession or overheating of the domestic economy
– interest rates changes in major foreign centres
– sizeable exchange rate movements, particularly if they threaten agreed bands in currency systems such as the European Exchange Rate Mechanism (ERM)
– major confidence changes triggering massive inflows or outflows of speculative capital.

It follows from the above list that the forecaster will need to monitor closely all the available evidence in domestic and international economic trends to gauge the likelihood of the authorities taking action to raise or lower interest rates. Two examples – one from the US, one from the UK – illustrate this.

In the US, the minutes of FOMC meetings (see Chap. 7), which are released a month after each meeting, are studied carefully to learn the Fed's current targets for money supply growth and the Fed funds rate. Observers then track how the money supply figures have performed against the Fed's target rates. If money supply has exceeded targets, a tightening of policy involving higher interest rates should be considered; if money supply has been below target, an easing of policy and lower interest rates are a possibility. However, as discussed in Chapter 7, such a conclusion is not inevitable because the Fed also has other priorities which it needs to address. For example, raising interest rates if the money supply overshoots may conflict with the need to ease the pain of recession in the domestic economy or, alternatively, may result in a strengthening of the dollar which may exacerbate international financial tensions.

In the UK, the performance of the exchange rate has assumed even greater prominence as an important key to interest rate movements since the pound entered the ERM in October 1990. The commitment to keep sterling within the agreed fluctuation band around its central rate against other currencies in the system introduces a powerful discipline when the value of the pound approaches its floor or ceiling. Consequently, the UK government's options with regard to interest rate policy are closely influenced by the need to keep the exchange rate within the agreed band. The factors which affect sterling's performance need to be carefully monitored, to give an indication of the future course of interest rate movements. The forecaster will, therefore, closely observe indicators such as money supply growth, inflation performance relative to other major economies, balance of payments developments on both current and capital accounts, major commodity price movements and the market's tolerance regarding the 'permitted' gap between, say, sterling and Deutschmark rates. Equally importantly, though more difficult to quantify, will be the assessment of confidence factors, such as geo-political developments in the Gulf or Eastern Europe, or the impact of a general election. If any factor seems likely to move sterling near its upper or lower limits, there will be implications for interest rates. According to the current ERM rules, the authorities are formally expected to take action, either through intervention on the foreign exchanges or an appropriate interest rate movement, when their currency hits its floor or ceiling against any one of the other member currencies or reaches the so-called divergence threshold, i.e. when the currency reaches 75% of its fluctuation margin against the European Currency Unit (ECU).

Other factors, particularly unemployment and the state of the domestic economy, are also highly relevant when the authorities consider interest rate policy. However, if there is an apparent conflict between the ERM commitment and domestic economic factors, the markets inevitably examine the strength of the government's commitment to the ERM and its willingness to incur political unpopularity to sustain sterling within the ERM bands.

Supply and demand factors

The supply of funds in the short-term analysis is determined by the day-to-day operations of the monetary authority (i.e. the central bank) through its management of the money market, as explained in Chapter 7. These operations are dictated by the need to avoid shortages or excesses of liquidity in the system and, in doing so, to prevent extreme volatility in interest rates. In addition, the central bank's activities are determined by the overall stance of monetary policy.

The availability of credit from the financial system is a major influence on the supply of funds in the economy. This, is turn, depends on the capital and liquidity position of the banking system, and the extent of any official controls on bank lending. However, it also depends on confidence factors, particularly the willingness of financial institutions to accept the unavoidable risks associated with credit expansion.

The demand for funds depends on the requirements for consumption and investment spending, as well as the borrowing ability of companies, private individuals and the public sector. These could reflect shocks to the system resulting from financial or political events which impact on income and wealth, either directly or through their effect on confidence. In addition, cyclical pressures in the economy, as reflected in the surpluses or deficits of the various sectors identified in the flow of funds analysis, will affect the demand/supply balance for funds which will in turn affect interest rates. The government's borrowing requirement (the PSBR) can be similar in size to the net financial position of any other sector, but is often more prominent in determining interest rate movements. For example, the emergence of a larger-than-expected budget deficit would tend to put upward pressure on interest rates, particularly at the long end, as the government's needs for additional funds to finance its borrowing requirement would intensify competition for available funds.

Market expectations

These demand and supply factors affect interest rates through their interaction with market expectations. Market participants, whether traders or investors, form views about both the direct impact of developments as well as the authorities' reaction to these events, and act on them – for example, by altering the distribution within their portfolios of assets with different periods to maturity. The immediate response to any development which impacts on interest rate expectations is to alter the shape of the yield curve, and involves changes in the level of interest rates at different points of the maturity spectrum. The

96

yield curve, properly interpreted, can closely reflect market views about future trends in interest rates, and can itself be used as a predictive tool though a rather imperfect one. The shape of the yield curve does not, in itself, tell us how prospective interest rates are made up as between inflation and real rates, and considerable judgement is needed in separating these two factors. There is no evidence to suggest that the yield curve is a better predictor of interest rates than individual forecasters or econometric models. The empirical evidence on this is likely to remain rather inconclusive. Even so, the yield curve will remain a key analytical tool for understanding and measuring expectations, and will always be a vital source of information to people actively trading in the markets.

Factors to consider in the long-term forecast

The further ahead the forecasting period extends, the greater is the emphasis placed on underlying trends; and the smaller is the ultimate significance of short-term, official responses to specific events or developments. Longer-term predictions inevitably lack the immediacy which can characterize very short-term forecasts, but they are also less susceptible to violent fluctuations. Therefore, although they rely on less information, longer-term forecasts are not necessarily either less accurate or less valuable than short-term ones. When looking ahead a year or more, the forecaster's chief objective is to predict the broad trends in, and approximate future level of, interest rates, rather than the precise timing of changes or the exact magnitude of short-term fluctuations. There are two elements that are most usefully considered when undertaking a longer-term forecast: the future rate of inflation and the fundamental forces likely to determine the real rate of interest.

Inflation

The factors which are examined in forecasting a country's rate of inflation (one of the variables on which the nominal rate of interest crucially depends) are all closely related to the underlying policy framework. This framework must be regarded as a key determinant of both the past record and the future prospects of a country's inflation performance. The fundamental importance of the policy framework reflects the fact that inflation, although affected by external factors such as wars or oil shocks, is ultimately due to policy mismanagement and, therefore, can be addressed through corrective actions. In the context of recent UK history, despite repeated commitments and undertakings by governments across the political spectrum to achieve better control of inflation, performance has been mediocre; and the UK has clearly shown a greater tolerance of, or proclivity to, inflation than countries such as Germany and Switzerland. In the past 30 years, UK inflation has averaged 7.7% per annum, compared with 5% in the US and only 3.4% in Germany. These long-term track records will strongly influence the thinking of market participants and of commentators about future inflation rates. However, it is important to appreciate that important policy changes can occasionally occur, and one such change may now be taking place in the UK.

Table 10.2 shows that France's entry into the ERM in 1979 has transformed, within a decade, the country's relative inflation performance. The gap between the French and German rates of inflation has been virtually eliminated. Indeed, over the next few years, French inflation could well be a little lower than the German rate. Sterling's entry into the ERM in 1990 could have a similarly profound beneficial impact on the UK's inflation rate. This is important because Britain's inflation rate must come down to the German level, and preferably fall below it for a few years, if sterling's entry into the ERM is to operate successfully. The credibility of the British government's anti-inflation commitment will be tested over the next few years, and there are now realistic hopes that a lasting reduction in the UK's long-term rate of inflation can indeed be achieved. Our current forecast of UK inflation is based on the expectation that, although it will initially remain above the German rate, there will be gradual and steady convergence between the two. This will be partly as a result of the UK's own adjustment to an environment of lower inflation, and partly because the massive costs of unification will result in a medium-term rise in German inflation. We also expect US inflation to average 4% in the 1990s, lower than its long-term average of 5% and

Table 10.2   Three decades of inflation among major economies

% per annum	1960–79	1980–89	1988–91	1992–96*
France	6.3	7.3	3.2	3.6
Germany	3.7	2.9	2.6	3.8
Japan	7.2	2.5	2.4	3.3
Switzerland	4.0	3.3	4.1	3.7
UK	7.9	7.4	7.0	4.1
US	4.7	5.5	4.7	4.0
OECD	5.8	5.9	4.6	4.1

*Forecast for the annual average over 5-year period 1992–96

in line with our general expectation of greater international convergence in inflation rates.

The next two factors considered are those that affect the real rate of interest: the stance of monetary policy; and the balance between the demand for and supply of savings.

Monetary policy

Short-term rates are largely determined by the authorities' monetary policy objectives and the instruments used to achieve them. However, it is important to appreciate that the authorities cannot simultaneously control money supply and interest rates. If the main policy focus is money supply as in the application of monetarist principles, the authorities have to accept the level of interest rates consistent with their money supply objectives. On the other hand, in a framework which aims more directly at controlling the level of interest rates, money supply growth becomes residual. Whereas interest rates in low inflation economies such as Germany and Switzerland have been consistently positive in real terms, in Britain and the US there have been considerable swings, with real interest rates moving from positive in the 1960s to negative in the 1970s and back to positive in the 1980s, in line with varying economic conditions and changing responses. The high real rates seen in the 1980s in the UK have persisted into the early 1990s, reflecting the tight policy stance adopted by the government. However, in the US where the threat of inflation has eased, there was significant relaxation in the early 1990s in response to fears about both the fragility of the financial system and short-term recessionary pressures. In making a long-range forecast regarding the course of short-term interest rates, it is crucial to decide whether official policy will remain tight, or whether – and to what extent – the authorities will feel able to reduce rates, as the threat of inflation subsides or as other concerns become more dominant. As mentioned already, in the UK's case a key factor will be the pound's performance in the ERM. If the UK succeeds in reducing inflation towards the average prevailing in the core ERM economies, nominal levels of short-term rates will fall, but real rates will still remain positive and reasonably high.

Demand/supply balance

Turning to long-term interest rates, it has already been established that the capacity of the authorities to exert a powerful direct influence in this area is limited. The level of, and movements in, short-term real interest rates have some influence on long-term rates, but the principal determinants of longer-term maturities are the demand/supply balance for funds, and expectations about government policy and the future rate of inflation. The relative importance of the various influences can change over time in response to, on the one hand, factors such as income, wealth, and the age structure of the population and, on the other hand, changes in perception of government policy and other factors determining the inflationary environment.

The relatively high level of real long-term rates currently prevailing reflects the perception that future demand for capital will be strong relative to the likely supply of savings. Significant contributors to this excess demand are the very large US and German budget deficits. However, other factors are also responsible. Developments in Eastern Europe generally have increased the prospective need for funds from OECD countries. In addition, German unification has sharply cut net savings in what used to be West Germany. The requirements of the Third World are a continuing potential claim on the supply of savings, and the global need for massive investment to deal with environmental concerns is likely to increase in importance. The impact of these factors will not abate, but one should not exaggerate the upward pressure on real interest rates emanating from these sources. In spite of their large requirements, neither Eastern Europe nor the Third World can bid for the capital they need in the market, and some of the funds they require will not be forthcoming. Indeed, while fears in some quarters of a major world recession are unduly pessimistic, one should not ignore the possible downward pressure on rates resulting from the unduly low money supply growth now being registered in many countries, notably the US. On balance, we expect the pattern of moderately high real long-term rates to continue in the next few years, because budget deficits will be sizeable and most major economies will persevere with firm anti-inflation policies. Our view is that over the next economic cycle, of say 4–5 years, the real long-term rate of interest in the OECD area will average around 4%. A comparison with rates prevailing in previous economic cycles is shown in Figures 10.1 and 10.2, which charts the real rates of interest in four major economies from 1973 to 1989 (1982–89 in the case of Japan). These diagrams show real interest rates rising to particularly high levels in the early- to mid-1980s. Nominal rates increased very sharply in 1979/80 in all four major economies shown, to cope with the inflationary consequences of the second oil price shock which coincided with general overheating as the economic cycle reached a peak. Subsequently, inflation fell sharply until about 1986, but nominal interest rates declined more slowly, reflecting the authorities' determination not to allow monetary easing to rekindle inflationary pressures.

100

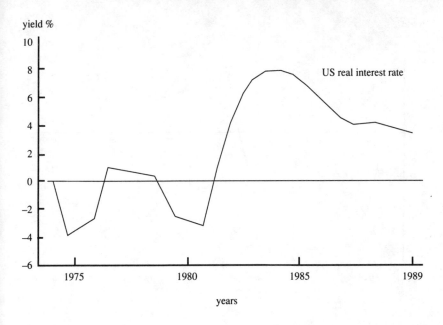

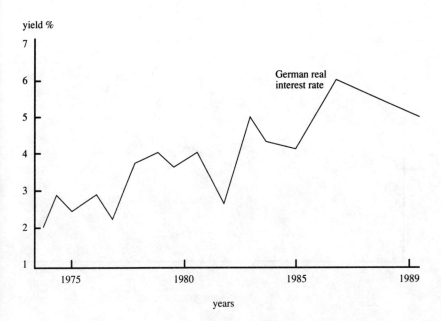

Figure 10.1 Real interest rates 1973–89 in the US, UK and Germany

101

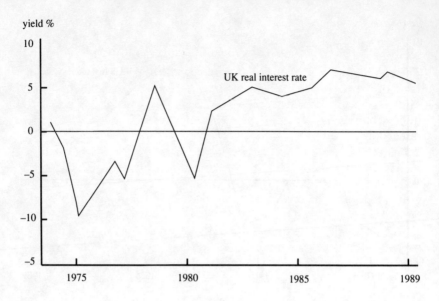

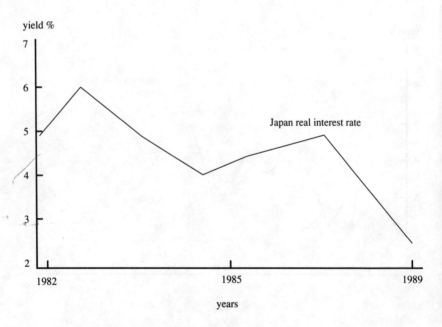

Figure 10.2 Real interest rates in the UK and Japan

The economic cycle

The consideration of interest rate patterns over the long term raises the issue of the relevance of the economic cycle to the analysis of interest rate movements. Interest rates vary appreciably over the cycle, as discussed in the next chapter. This section lays the groundwork for that discussion.

Figure 10.3 shows that, although the exceptionally sharp volatility seen in the last century and in the 1920s and 1930s has been reduced, the cycle is still a continuing feature of economic life. Real GNP does not grow at a steady pace, but is subject to quite sharp swings. After a period of expansion, bottlenecks and pressures impose strains on capacity (usually manifested in worsening inflation and balance of payments problems) and action is then required to reduce overheating. This can lead eventually to a period of slow or even negative growth, before recovery commences and the renewed growth phase takes the economy to a new peak, or upper turning point in the cycle.

Given the close integration of major countries within the world economy, it is to be expected that their economic cycles will coincide fairly often. Figure 10.3 indicates a fairly close synchronization between the economic cycles of Germany and the US in recent decades. One important recent exception was in 1990/91, when the US experienced a fairly shallow recession while Germany continued to experience strong growth largely due to unification effects. This disparity in cyclical movements was reflected in a strong divergence between falling US interest rates and rises in Germany. Japan showed great cyclical volatility in the 1960s, with growth rates ranging from 5% to almost 15%, but growth has been much steadier in the past 15 years. The Japanese cycle has usually been closely synchronized with those of the US and Germany, particularly in the last two decades. Figure 10.4 illustrates the close synchronization of the economic cycle in major European countries.

Conclusion

In this chapter we have discussed the fundamental factors to take into account in forecasting interest rates. The expected rate of inflation is crucial in determining nominal rates; but to complete the analysis one must assess the factors affecting real interest rates. Knowledge of these fundamental factors does not make it easy to forecast interest rates, nor does it ensure the accuracy of the result, since the factors have

103

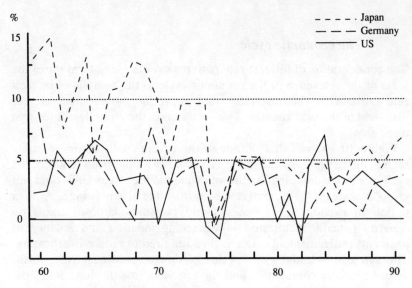

Figure 10.3 World growth rates 1960–90

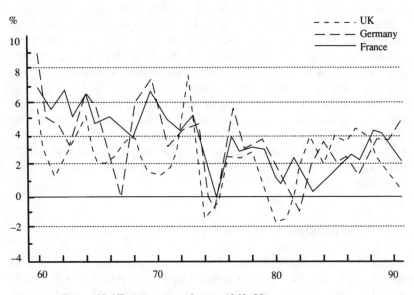

Figure 10.4 European growth rates 1960–90

themselves to be forecast. However, knowledge of the key variables on which interest rates depend is an essential starting point in the analysis. The application of the framework provided by an understanding of these variables is presented in the next chapter.

CHAPTER 11

Forecasting techniques

The conceptual framework and the key ingredients for analysing interest rate movements were considered in the previous chapter. We now move on to the practical aspects of forecasting. There are essentially two approaches. The approach with which we are primarily concerned identifies the fundamental factors underlying interest rate movements and uses these within an economic model, either structured or informal. The second approach, sometimes referred to as technical analysis or 'chartism', is purely a statistical framework for analysing various market features and drawing conclusions from them about short-term trends. Although both approaches are used in the business world we do not regard them as equivalent alternatives. Only the fundamental approach attempts to provide a logical analytical framework for understanding the basic relationships.

The fundamental approach

The fundamental approach is based on a formal or informal economic model incorporating linkages among the various factors influencing interest rate changes. Such a model might be 'structured', using mathematical representations of relationships between variables. Alternatively, the model might be an informal 'mental' one, where the forecaster analyses and attempts to quantify the range of economic influences, but where the complexity of the relationships cannot be expressed through a mathematical equation.

As previous chapters have shown, many factors which in theory are relevant to interest rate forecasting can be included in the model, whether structured or mental. We have dealt in some detail with these factors: the rate of inflation; the economic cycle; government policy; the

106

demand for capital and the supply of savings; the framework provided by flow of funds analysis; the exchange rate, and market expectations of official action. In addition, there are certain structural factors – important events which can radically affect the outlook, either permanently or over a period – which need to be taken into account. One recent example is German unification, which has exerted appreciable pressure on Germany's impressive inflation performance. Another example was France's decision to join the ERM, a move which persuaded the French authorities to place a high priority on controlling inflation and to accept slower growth and higher unemployment during much of the 1980s. After a decade of improving inflation performance and several years of exchange rate stability against the Deutschmark, French interest rates have moved virtually into line with those of Germany, a development which has been helped over the past two years by the impact of Germany's own structural change. This convergence of interest rates over the past decade, stemming from two basically unrelated structural changes, is illustrated in Figure 11.1.

Such structural shifts, and their interaction with the fundamental factors mentioned earlier, need to be taken into account in the forecasting process. However, it can readily be appreciated that to incorporate all this information, involving the use of many behavioural equations and variables, results in a macro-economic financial model which is complex and unwieldy. The informal mental model, although

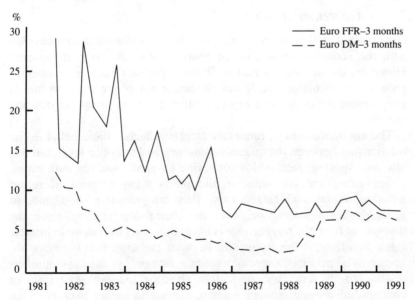

Figure 11.1 French and German rates 1981–91

more flexible, will still find it difficult to handle all the data simultaneously. At different times, different factors will appear to have greater
influence. In practice, however, for purposes of forecasting interest
rates beyond a very short-term time horizon (and, incidentally, the
technical analysis only has value for very short-term forecasts), the
following factors – as indicated in the matrix for interest rate forecasting
shown in Chapter 10 – will always feature prominently:

– government policy
– the economic cycle
– inflation performance
– longer term demand/supply factors.

This chapter will focus on a practical approach to forecasting techniques. The following comments on each of these four factors are
intended to throw light on some important relationships which can be
used in attempting to forecast interest rates. The factors are considered
separately in order to highlight their particular features, but in practice
they are inter-related to a considerable degree. To give just one
example: government policy affects the timing of turning points in the
economic cycle, while the cyclicality of economic performance will
influence key policy decisions.

Government policy

Government policy, as we have just noted, is closely interconnected
with the economic cycle and, of course, with inflation performance.
However, the authorities may well have specific targets for monetary
growth, the exchange rate and public sector borrowing, and this makes
government policy *per se* a key variable in the interest rate forecasting
model.

The announcement of monetary targets reflects a basic belief in the
relationship between the quantity of money and the price level, but it is
also an important method for conveying a signal about the authorities'
policy aims, and for reducing the public's expectations of future
inflation. Where such targets exist, they can provide a good guide to
official policy actions to influence short-term interest rates, since any
divergence from the target range is likely to be met by a move in interest
rates. Similarly, if the authorities have an exchange rate target or are
known to be pursuing a specific exchange rate policy, any developments
relating to the fundamental factors affecting the exchange rate, or
changes influencing foreign exchange dealers' views, may need an
interest rate response. Government policy relating to public sector

borrowing is also important, in so far as the size and financing of the borrowing requirement are important determinants of money supply growth and may thus have an indirect effect on interest rates. The size of the borrowing requirement also has a direct impact on long-term interest rates. Thus, if government actions seem likely to produce an overshoot of borrowing requirement expectations or target, a rise in long-term interest rates is a strong possibility.

Among the possible policy targets mentioned above, an exchange rate target normally provides the most powerful discipline. It is not surprising, therefore, that within much of Europe, adherence to the ERM discipline has emerged as the effective and powerful policy instrument for securing monetary stability.

The economic cycle

The close connection between the economic cycle and movements in interest rates was mentioned briefly in Chapter 10, and we now focus more closely on this important relationship. One can look upon the economic cycle as the key factor determining demand/supply factors in the money market with a time horizon of about 12–18 months, and it is one of the main triggers for official policy reactions. An illustrative theoretical framework is summarized in Figure 11.2.

As the economic cycle reaches its peak, there is mounting evidence of

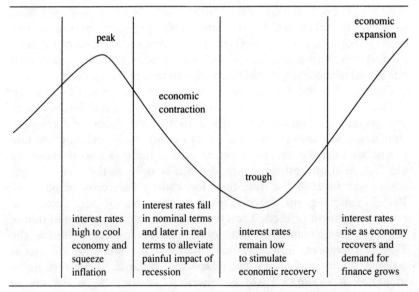

Figure 11.2 A theoretical framework of the economic cycle

overheating in the economy. Buoyant consumer demand causes infla-tionary pressure and, in most countries, this is accompanied by a widening current account deficit on the balance of payments. In reaction, the authorities take restrictive monetary action, mainly by raising real interest rates. Fiscal policy may also be tightened at this stage of the cycle. For the next few quarters, interest rates remain high to ensure that excess demand is dampened and inflation is forced out of the system. This is normally an unpleasant process resulting in produc-tion falling and the number of jobless rising. Once it is clear that inflation is decelerating other priorities emerge. In order to alleviate the painful effects of the economic recession, the level of interest rates is gradually reduced. Initially, inflation tends to fall more sharply than interest rates and real rates are actually rising but, after a few months, the decline in rates becomes more pronounced and the level of real interest rates comes down at that stage. Finally, in order to assist economic recovery, interest rates are kept low at the trough of the cycle and during the initial upswing of the economy. Indeed, in the early stages of the next upturn, real interest rates continue to fall, as inflation rises while nominal interest rates remain low.

The above mechanistic description of the relationship between the economic cycle and interest rates is naturally subject to many variations. It must also be stressed that the changes in interest rates are normally triggered by the monetary authority, particularly at the short end of the maturity spectrum. However, the interest rates quoted by financial institutions and, indeed, the central bank's own actions are also significantly influenced by demand/supply pressures in the money market. For example, a sharp reduction in demand for lending during a cyclical downturn would be a significant signal to both the commercial banks and to those responsible for policy to reduce interest rates.

Figures 11.3 and 11.4 examine the performance over the past two decades of the UK and US economies, in terms of real interest rates and economic growth. The charts show that the theoretical relation-ship described above between the economic cycle and interest rate levels has been borne out in practice over the past two decades. In the UK, real interest rates turned down sharply as the recession got under way in 1974 and remained low during the recovery phase of 1975/76, moving up sharply towards the end of the decade as economic growth peaked. The cycle was then broadly repeated during the 1981 trough and the next two years of recovery. During the 1990/92 recession, however, real interest rates failed to decline as significantly as might have been expected, because of the restraining influence of sterling's ERM membership. In the US, as we saw in Chapter 10, real rates were very low during the 1970s, but still moved

110

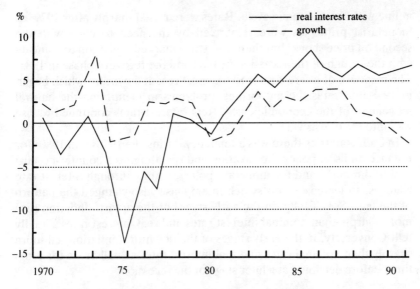

Figure 11.3 UK growth and real interest rates 1970–91

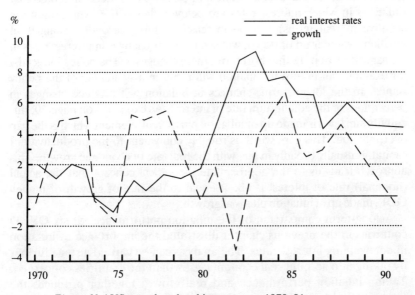

Figure 11.4 US growth and real interest rates 1970–91

in line with the economic cycle. Rates were raised sharply after 1979, as monetarist principles were reinforced by the need to cope with the second oil price shock, but there was still a marked reduction to coincide with the trough of the recession in 1982 and the recovery phase in 1983. The response of interest rates to the most recent downturn which began in 1988 illustrates the authorities' problems in identifying the natural movement of the economic cycle. Real interest rates continued to rise well into the downswing.

In both countries there was a tendency during the 1970s and 1980s for reliance on fiscal policy, i.e.taxation and spending, as a counter-cyclical tool to diminish; and for monetary policy, mainly through interest rate changes, to increase. This switch in emphasis also changed the pattern of the lags. Specifically, in the early stages of the upturn, inflation rose more sharply than nominal interest rates and real interest rates actually fell. Conversely, in the early stages of the downturn, inflation fell more sharply than nominal rates and real interest rates actually rose for some time, before declining at a later stage of the recession.

Inflation performance

Inflation is a key factor in two important respects. Firstly, it provides an effective 'floor' to the level of interest rates, since it is widely accepted that situations in which interest rates are below inflation (i.e. where they are negative in real terms) will be increasingly rare. Secondly, changes in inflation, whether up or down, will often trigger changes in interest rates in the same direction. In the short term, these changes will be policy-induced – for example, an upturn in inflation will result in a tightening of the policy stance. In the longer term, changes in inflation will produce changes in perceptions of the equilibrium rate of interest. As explained on page 20, this equilibrium level is made up of inflation plus a 'real' element which is the gap over inflation. This gap, which is roughly equivalent to the productivity of capital, is usually broadly in line with the real rate of economic growth. This approach leads us to the approximate theoretical concept that the actual (nominal) rate of interest is about equal to the rate of growth of money GDP, made up of inflation plus real growth.

A long-term comparison of the inflation performance for six OECD countries in the previous chapter illustrated the importance of inflation in determining interest rates. The analysis can be carried a stage further by taking into account real economic growth in the countries concerned. Taking inflation performance and real growth together produces the concept of change in money GDP, which as the figures show differs from the interest rate level in individual years, but bears a fairly close relationship to interest rate levels over 5-year periods, (Table 11.1).

Table 11.1   Change in money GDP in France, Germany and the UK

	France		Germany		UK	
	Money GDP	Interest rates	Money GDP	Interest rates	Money GDP	Interest rates
1981	12.1	18.0	4.3	11.7	10.2	13.9
1982	13.9	19.6	3.2	8.5	9.0	12.3
1983	10.3	16.3	5.4	5.5	9.3	10.1
1984	8.0	12.6	5.2	5.8	6.3	10.0
1985	7.9	10.7	4.3	5.3	9.8	12.2
1986	7.9	9.3	5.5	4.6	7.6	10.9
1987	5.7	8.5	3.4	4.0	9.9	9.7
1988	8.2	8.0	5.1	4.3	10.9	10.3
1989	7.5	9.3	6.5	7.0	9.1	13.9
1990	5.7	10.2	8.2	8.5	7.0	14.8
Ave. 81–85	10.4	15.4	4.5	7.4	8.9	11.7
86–90	7.0	9.1	5.7	5.7	8.9	11.9

Average % change over the previous year

Demand/supply factors

Interest rates are prices bringing demand and supply into equilibrium. Investment demands and the supply of loanable funds in the global economy, and in individual countries, will clearly have a material effect on domestic interest rates. For example, we mentioned in Chapter 10 the potential demand for finance from a number of important sources. If this demand cannot be matched by an increase in global savings, upward pressure on long-term interest rates will develop. Similarly, if the supply is subject to restriction, perhaps because of an increase in perception of risk by financial institutions, the same effect will be seen. These factors must be brought into the model.

Application of the model

In this section, we attempt a brief illustration of the model approach in practice by applying the basic principles considered in this chapter to the UK and US economies at the end of 1990 (Table 11.2 and Table 11.3). At the time of the forecast, December 1990, UK short-term rates (base rate) stood at 14%. Essentially, the forecast needed to consider how fast rates could come down given the conflicting pressures, domestic and external considerations, facing the government. Our view at the time was that 'the balance of economic factors points towards . . . modest base rate declines to 12% during the early months of 1991, without

113

Table 11.2   UK economic situation late 1990: implications for short-term interest rates

Factor	Comment	Impact on future interest rates
Government policy	Need to react to recession and falling inflation. M0 within target. But exchange rate stability within ERM a powerful consideration	Apparent conflict between domestic and external factors as many fear that ERM discipline will preclude falls in interest rates. In the event, confidence gained through ERM discipline permits a larger and faster fall in interest rates than would otherwise have been possible
Economic cycle	Economy in recession for two quarters. Unemployment rising rapidly	Nominal rates fall. Real interest rates initially fall more sharply than nominal rates
Inflation	At almost 11% year-on-year. Forecast to decline sharply to reach about 5% by end 1991	Allows a large reduction in nominal rates
Demand/supply factors	Demand for credit weak. Modest PSBR for 1990/91	Scope for reduction in rates
Structural factors	£ joined ERM in Oct 1990. Government determined to establish credibility	Need to consider interest rate differentials with other ERM members

endangering unduly sterling's position within the ERM'. Base rates were in fact cut to 12% by April and sterling remained stable within the ERM. The forecast for the rest of 1991 was that the opportunity for further cuts would be very limited given the probability of some tightening of policy in Germany. This view proved rather too pessimistic, since a further 1% cut in base rate was possible. The longer-term forecast was for base rate to fall to 10% by the end of 1992. However, as

Table 11.3 US economic situation late 1990: implications for short-term interest rates

Factor	Comment	Impact on future interest rates
Government policy	Policy easing to boost economy. M2 at lower end of target range	Scope for further reduction in rates
Economic cycle	Economy in recession; key indicators weak	Interest rates should fall in real terms
Inflation	High but easing	Nominal rates set to decline
Demand/supply factors	Budget deficit reduction package agreed	Could lead to a modest fall in long-term rates
Structural factors	Fragility of financial and real estate sectors posing serious risks	Pressure to reduce rates

confidence in the UK's ERM commitment improved our forecast was revised by September, to expect a fall to 9% by the end of 1991.

US prime rates in December 1990 stood at 10%. The forecast was for a decline to 9.5% in the first quarter of the year, in line with economic weakness, to alleviate problems in the financial and real estate sectors. Later in the year, as the US economy recovered, the forecast was for prime rates to rise again, reaching 10% by the end of 1992. Inflation fell more sharply than expected and, in the event, prime rates fell to 9% by March (0.5% more than forecast). The US economy showed signs of recovery during the second and early third quarters of 1991 and prime rates remained steady for a time. However, weak data raised fears that the recovery was petering out and led to a further steady easing of monetary conditions in the second half of the year, and prime rates fell further to 7.5% at the end of 1991.

Technical analysis

While the fundamentalist approach attempts to explain interest rate movements by using tested relationships between economic variables, technical analysis focuses entirely on trends in interest rates. It makes no attempt to look at the reasons underlying those trends, which are in themselves considered to encompass, and to have discounted, all the market forces balancing supply and demand.

Chart analysis is based on the idea that it is possible to identify recurring patterns in time series of data and, in particular, to predict short-term turning points. This is an area which the fundamental factors approach cannot always pronounce on, since it is based on a consideration of underlying trends which are likely to become apparent only over a medium- or long-term time horizon.

Although the chartist approach has been criticized for its lack of a firm theoretical foundation, it is widely used for short-term forecasts, though there is as yet no systematic evidence of the quality of the forecasts produced by the approach. Moreover, chartism is an important factor forming market expectations (especially in the foreign exchange markets, since its findings are widely believed and acted upon, and therefore exert a direct influence on rates). Recognition of chartist results is therefore a useful complement to fundamental analysis, especially in short-term forecasts and in the analysis of expectations.

Practitioners of technical analysis employ a variety of analytical tools

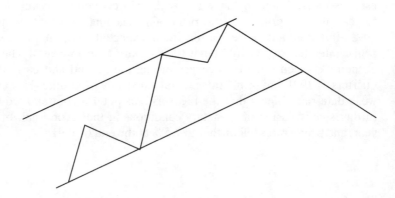

Figure 11.5 Trend lines

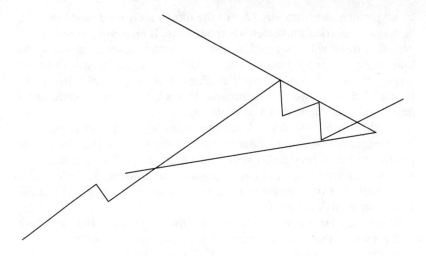

Figure 11.6 Break out

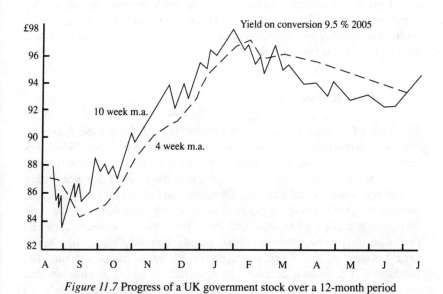

Figure 11.7 Progress of a UK government stock over a 12-month period

117

to aid pattern identification. One of the most widely used to identify the direction of market movements is trend lines. If rates are plotted over a period, a trend will emerge. Chartists will connect a series of highs and lows along the trend (possibly using moving-averages to smooth short-term volatilities) within parallel lines (see Fig. 11.5). If, as in Figure 11.5, the lower line is broken, this would be an indication of a possible change in the direction of the market.

Another technique is to identify triangles where, for example, rate movements can be seen to moderate after a sharp rise or fall, and can be plotted within a triangle as shown in Figure 11.6. The 'break out' is always a strong movement either upwards or downwards, reflecting a continuation of the upward trend in this example, or a reversal had the break out been downward.

There are a large number of other chartists techniques, but the nature of the analysis should be clear from these examples. A practical example of this approach is shown in Figure 11.7 which charts the progess over a 12-month period of a UK government stock, Conversion 9.5% 2005. This is charted in terms of its price, but since the yield varies inversely with the price, the interest rate implications are clear. The chart tracks actual price movements against 4- and 10-week moving averages. The latest observation (for early July 1991) shows the price breaking clear of both these moving averages, giving a clear indication to the analyst that long-term interest rates are due to fall.

Conclusion

The lack of a logical foundation can be regarded as a weakness of chartism. So too can the subjectivity of much of the analysis. Nevertheless, this approach has many adherents among market practitioners, and its track record in short-term forecasting is neither better nor worse than that of the fundamental analysis. Chartism can indeed play a significant, though temporary, role in practice since many operators act on their own interpretation of trends, and these self-fulfilling expectations can over a period produce the short-term results they are forecasting. As the time horizon of the forecast lengthens, there is no doubt that the fundamental approach becomes more suitable, and it is unlikely that forecasters or decision-makers will rely on a chartist approach for periods longer than a few weeks. The amount of space devoted in this book to a consideration of the factors affecting interest rate movements reflects the dominance of the fundamental approach for longer-term forecasts. Chapter 12 uses this approach to provide a forecast of international rate movements over the next five years.

CHAPTER 12

Interest rates in the 1990s

In this chapter, we bring together some of the principles and concepts discussed earlier and apply them in a practical exercise, to help form a view of the likely course of interest rates in the 1990s. We shall not attempt to make specific numerical forecasts for precise dates. Periodic economic reports, in which the specific numbers can be reviewed regularly, are a more appropriate vehicle for detailed forecasting than a book which largely focuses on basic principles. Moreover, the 10-year timescale, in which many circumstances can change, is too long for very specific numerical projections. At the same time, however, the inter-action between the basic relevant factors and their impact can often be best understood over a long period. Our aim in this chapter is, therefore, to identify the key forces likely to determine the general trend of UK and international rates over the remainder of the decade, and to try and quantify their impact.

The real rate of interest

The long-term data described in Chapter 9 establish the historical background. In that chapter, the level of real interest rates in recent decades was examined for a number of countries in 5-year periods as shown Table 12.1. The table highlights a number of important features which form a useful guide for the forecast:

– real rates of interest averaged between 1% and 3.5% during the 1960s, a period of moderate inflation
– real rates were generally much lower in the 1970s than in the 1960s, and in some countries were negative. This low level of real rates, although initially a statistical result of a sudden upsurge in inflation,

119

Table 12.1   Real rates 1960–91

%	US	UK	Germany	Japan
1961–65	2.7	1.0	1.2	2.7
1966–70	3.0	2.2	3.4	2.0
1971–75	1.5	−4.7	1.4	−3.7
1976–80	0.6	−2.8	1.6	0.8
1981–85	6.2	3.5	3.7	4.4
1986–91	3.8	5.7	5.0	4.7
Ave. 1961–91	3.0	−0.8	2.7	1.8

became an important factor exacerbating inflationary pressures in its own right and making them more entrenched. This reflected the fact that policy during the 1970s became more concerned with countering recession, and was therefore more accommodating towards inflation

– in the 1980s, real interest rates were in general much higher than in the 1970s and also higher than in the 1960s. The 1980s saw a sharp reversal of some of the events and policy tendencies seen in the 1970s. Many governments adopted firm anti-inflation policies in the 1980s, and high real interest rates were not only a statistical consequence of lower inflation but, even more importantly, a basic policy tool aimed at sustaining a low-inflation environment.

At the end of the 1980s, there were welcome signs that inflationary pressures were subsiding in the UK and the US – countries where historically inflationary pressures were relatively strong. However, since these countries were entering recession, there was some uncertainty as to whether the lower level of inflation was a cyclical, and therefore temporary, situation or a more permanent development.

In the US, lower inflation during 1991 was accompanied by a very sharp drop in nominal interest rates. As it became increasingly clear during the year that economic recovery was not taking place and that the economy might even be sliding into a renewed recession, short-term interest rates were reduced very sharply to a point at which, by the end of 1991, real interest rates were not far above zero. In December the Federal Reserve's discount rate was at a 27-year low of 3.5%, while the annual rate of inflation was 3.1%. In the UK, nominal interest rates also fell during the recession (with base rates falling from 15% in October 1990 to 10.5% a year later). However, the UK's commitment to a stable pound in the ERM forced nominal UK interest rates to remain slightly above those in Germany, and real rates of interest remained exceptionally high at a time when the economy was still very weak and might have benefited from lower rates. Meanwhile, although the German economy also started to weaken, real rates in that country remained high, reflecting the costs of unification and the authorities' determination to curb inflation.

Looking ahead, there are two strong reasons for believing that real interest rates during the 1990s will remain positive throughout the OECD area, and will be relatively high in Europe but less so in the US and Japan. The first reason for assuming that real rates will not become negative again is that government policy in most OECD countries will continue to reflect a firm commitment to restraining inflation. This tendency will be reinforced in Europe by the determination of countries such as the UK, Italy and Spain to use relatively high interest rates to ensure that their currencies remain fairly stable within their ERM bands, and by the commitment of Germany to ensure that the inflationary pressures resulting from unification are contained through firm monetary policies. A return to the low or negative rates of interest seen during the 1970s is highly unlikely in the 1990s. At the same time, the successes already achieved in reducing inflation and the markets' increased confidence in the various governments' anti-inflation commitments will make it possible for the gap between interest rates and inflation to be lower than the punitive levels prevailing in recent years. This opportunity to reduce gradually the recent very high level of real interest rates will be reinforced by the pressure to ease the heavy debt burdens facing individuals and companies which are an overhang from the excesses of the 1980s.

The second reason for believing that real interest rates will remain at a higher level than in the 1970s is the demand/supply balance for funds in the global economy. As shown in Chapter 9, there has been a gradual but steady decline in the ratio of savings to GNP in the OECD area, in both the private and the public sectors, and this has tended to depress the supply of funds. Clearly savings worldwide must, by definition, be equal to investment for any period. However, this does not exclude the possibility that at a given price for savings (i.e. at a given interest rate) there may be a savings shortfall in relation to the demand for funds to invest, and that the shortfall can only be removed by an increase in price, i.e. a rise in the rate of interest, or by some form of rationing. It is possible that in the 1990s there may be occasional shortfalls but fears of a general global shortage of capital are exaggerated.

Both the industrialized and lesser developed countries continue to require large amounts of capital in order to finance massive long-term investment projects. The cost of absorbing East Germany has pushed the German fiscal deficit to some 5% of GNP. This factor alone could keep German domestic interest rates high for the next few years and, through ERM links, exert an upward influence on other European rates. In addition, demands for development finance from the newly emerging former Comecon bloc in Eastern Europe and from the new ex-Soviet republics are enormous. Even more important are the financing requirements stemming from the growing pressure for industry to adapt to increasingly demanding and costly environmental factors. There is also the cost of rebuilding decaying infrastructures in many industrialized countries; and the continuing demands of developing countries in Latin America, Africa and Asia for development funds. The market place will ultimately decide which among these competing demands will succeed and on what time scale. Clearly, not all needs will be satisfied in the next few years. Nevertheless, sizeable effective demand relative to supply will ensure that pressure on real interest rates remains strong.

In our view, this combination of policy and the demand/supply balance will result in real interest rates averaging 2.5–4.5% in the OECD countries during the first half of the 1990s. However, there will be scope for real rates to fall gradually to a range of 2–3% in the second half of the decade with growing market confidence in a more stable policy framework which lessens the risk of renewed inflationary excesses, and as a gradual increase in the private sector savings ratio reduces the shortfall between investment demand and the supply of savings.

Inflation and the nominal rate of interest

Having formed a view about the outlook for real interest rates in the 1990s, we can now turn to forecast nominal interest rates, which will clearly depend on the prospects for inflation. There are good reasons to believe that inflation in the OECD area will remain moderate. Governments will continue to place a high priority on controlling inflation, and it seems rather unlikely that we will experience major shocks to the economic system similar to the first oil crisis of 1973/74. There is a greater awareness worldwide that a degree of exchange rate stability is desirable. This is particularly true in Europe, where there is a strong movement towards full economic and monetary union (EMU) based on the firm promise of monetary stability along the lines applied successfully over many years by the Bundesbank. However, even at a global level there is a strong view that a degree of co-ordination (although not a fixed exchange rate system) between the dollar, the yen and the European currencies is desirable.

At the same time, there is no realistic prospect that inflation can be completely eliminated from the economic system, or even kept permanently at a 1–2% level. The existence of major imbalances, such as the impact of German unification, the persistence of large-scale problems arising from huge indebtedness and over-blown asset prices in the US and Japan, lead us to the view that in the medium term inflation will average some 4% per annum in most major industrialized economies. Historic trends and the outlook for inflation are summarized below:

OECD inflation 1960–99 (%) per annum
1960–79: 6.0
1980–89: 5.9
1990–99: 3.8

The combination of inflation at around 4% and real interest rates of 2.5–3.5% will result in nominal short-term rates averaging around 6.5–7.5% in the OECD area until the mid-1990s. Specifically, we expect US and Japanese rates to average 6.5% in the next few years and German rates to average 7.5%. In the second half of the decade, inflation will edge down towards 3%, resulting in nominal interest rates easing towards an average level of 5.5–6.5%. Longer-term interest rates will be on average some 1% higher than short rates, though, as already explained, the gap between long and short rates will vary over the economic cycle.

Finally, the level of UK interest rates over the coming decade will depend crucially on the ability of the economy to converge to the harsh discipline of a lower inflation environment in the ERM and, in the longer term, in full EMU. UK inflation in early 1992 is virtually identical to that in Germany; but, given that the UK recession is appreciably worse than Germany's, it is plausible to argue that underlying inflation is still probably somewhat higher. The acid test of the UK's ability to adjust smoothly and relatively painlessly to the requirements of the ERM is the speed with which labour costs fall to a level which is consistent with an inflation rate of at most 4%. While such a reduction is achievable, and will in our view occur, it will necessitate a period of higher real interest rates than in other major OECD countries. Our current forecast suggests that UK short-term nominal rates will average 8.5% in the next five years, coming down to 6–6.5% in the second half of the decade, as the inflation gap between the UK and its major partners shrinks.

CHAPTER 13

The value and dangers of forecasting

Economic and financial forecasting has expanded very rapidly over the past two decades. Although the rapid pace of change in the financial markets has resulted in exceptionally large forecasting errors, particularly in areas such as interest rates and currencies, the demand for systematic projections, both short- and long-term, seems set to continue expanding. There can be little doubt that governments as well as business enterprises must evaluate future trends in order to make sensible decisions. At the same time, it is pertinent to assess in a realistic manner what is the most effective way in which efforts to forecast market-determined variables (such as interest rates) provide genuine help to the business planner or the decision maker on economic policy.

It is useful to start by clearing up a number of fallacies and misconceptions that cause misunderstandings amongst those involved in either making or using forecasts. Firstly, forecasters often fail to stress that specific projections are only logical deductions based on assumptions – either about the external environment or about the underlying relationships involved – which the people undertaking the exercise regard as 'reasonable'. Clearly, different assumptions about economic and political factors and their inter-relationships, perhaps equally reasonable, will produce different forecasts. Secondly, recipients of economic forecasts too often confuse a forecast with an unattainable prophesy. Consequently, such recipients are naturally disappointed in their search for an elixir and go to the other extreme, taking the highly dangerous view that, since forecasts are often wrong, one can manage without them.

Admittedly, forecasts do not need to be made by specialized units. Decision-makers – a chief executive, or a finance director – may on occasion produce more accurate projections of future trends than the professional forecaster. However, the essential point is that business decisions will always require a logical framework of assumptions and projections about key variables such as sales, costs, interest rates and currency values. One key question is whether these forecasts are explicit or implicit ('seat of the pants'), and whether they are made by professional staff trained in economics, statistics and related disciplines. The larger and more complex the decisions being made, the greater the need for an explicit and systematic forecasting framework. This is usually best undertaken by a team of specialists which is not involved directly in day-to-day operational decisions, and which is therefore better able to offer an objective and realistic assessment of the available options.

Since so many forecasts have turned out to be violently wrong, it is not surprising that, notwithstanding the continued growth in the demand for the services of forecasters, users have become rather cynical about economists – the professionals most closely involved with forecasting – and their usefulness. As we have tried to explain, some of this cynicism is a function of misunderstanding on the part of both providers and users of forecasts. Consistent accuracy is a fair test for the usefulness of a forecast. However, spurious or freak accuracy of one number in an exercise which might involve projections of about 100 variables or more is not particularly helpful.

The only real test of a competent forecast is whether it provides the decision maker with a logical and coherent mental framework for a realistic valuation of options, which will enhance systematically, and over time, the quality of the decisions taken. Once it is understood that a forecast cannot be a prophecy, one will also appreciate that a forecaster cannot take over the final responsibility from the person who ultimately has to make the decision.

Many forecasters, faced with the virtual certainty that they will occasionally be proved wrong, tend to use a number of devices in order to avoid embarrassment. They might give a very wide range for their projections: for example, saying that base rate at the end of the year will be in a range of 8%–12% or that the dollar/sterling exchange rate will be in a range of $1.50–$2.00. Such a wide range will obviously increase the chances of getting it right, but will also make the whole exercise virtually meaningless. Another well-established technique is to use 'scenario analysis' in order to cater for a whole variety of possible events: for example, global economic trends, election results or developments in the oil/commodity markets. If used sensibly and in a focused manner, scenario analysis can be helpful in exploring the different implications of major trends or events such as general elections, wars or energy crises. However, indiscriminate and large-scale use of scenarios involves a huge computational burden in producing and digesting numerous possible outcomes. Clearly, this technique should be used very selectively, and only when dealing with major identifiable events.

Our clear preference when presenting a forecast is to make sure that the recipients fully understand the limitations of any forecasting exercise, and then to provide them with explicit numerical projections. The linkages between the underlying assumptions and the specific numerical projections are clearly stated and where possible we try to explain how a change in assumptions will alter the forecasts. We fully recognize the dangers of the spurious accuracy which can be attached to numerical forecasts. However, the underlying economic uncertainties must not be a reason for lack of clarity in presentation. We strongly believe that explicit forecasts (particularly of interest and exchange rates), based on clearly stated assumptions about the underlying economic environment, are the most useful way of communicating risks and uncertainties to those making decisions.

Index

INDEX

money supply, 5, 47, 48, 50, 84, 89, 99
   targets, 46, 47, 48, 77, 83, 87, 94–5,
     108
Moody's, 42

National Savings Certificates, 27

oil shocks, 74, 77, 80, 97
open market operations, 49, 50, 54–6, 57
Organisations of Petroleum Exporting
    Countries (OPEC), 23, 74, 80

pattern identification, 118
prime rates, 115
purchasing power parity (PPP) 63–5

real theories of interest, 2–4
redemption yield, 29
repurchase agreements (repos), 57
risk, 30, 32–3, 35, 40–4
   country risk, 43

Smithsonian Conference, 74
Standard & Poor's, 42

technical analysis, 106, 116–18

Vietnam War, 74
Volcker, Paul, 24, 80

yield curve, 17, 29–39, 96–7